Saunders
Physical
Activities
Series

Edited by

MARYHELEN VANNIER, Ed.D.

Professor and Director, Women's Division,
Department of Health and Physical Education,
Southern Methodist University

HOLLIS F. FAIT, Ph.D.

Professor of Physical Education,
School of Physical Education,
University of Connecticut

THIRD EDITION

BOWLING

Carol Schunk

Exercise Therapist

ILLUSTRATED BY JAMES BONNER

 SAUNDERS COLLEGE PUBLISHING

Philadelphia New York Chicago
San Francisco Montreal Toronto
London Sydney Tokyo Mexico City
Rio de Janeiro Madrid

Address orders to:
383 Madison Avenue
New York, NY 10017

Address editorial correspondence to:
West Washington Square
Philadelphia, PA 19105

This book was set in Press Roman by TechType Graphics.
The editors were John Butler and Lynne Gery.
The art & design director was Richard L. Moore.
The text design was done by Phoenix Studio, Inc.
The cover design was done by Richard L. Moore.
The production manager was Maureen Read.

Cover credit: Artwork drawn by Tom Mallon.

Library of Congress Cataloging in Publication Data

Schunk, Carol.
   Bowling.
   (Saunders physical activity series)
   Bibliography: p.
   1. Bowling. I. Title. II. Series.

GV903.S36 1983   794.6   82-60634

ISBN 0-03-062447-9

BOWLING   ISBN 0-03-062447-9

2345 090 987654321

CBS COLLEGE PUBLISHING
Saunders College Publishing
Holt, Rinehart and Winston
The Dryden Press

EDITORS' FOREWORD

Every period of history, as well as every society, has its own profile. Our own world of the last third of the twentieth century is no different. Whenever we step back to look at ourselves, we can see excellences and failings, strengths and weaknesses, that are peculiarly ours.

One of our strengths as a nation is that we are a sports-loving people. Today more persons — and not just young people — are playing, watching, listening to, and reading about sports and games. Those who enjoy themselves most are the men and women who actually *play* the game: the "doers."

You are reading this book now for either of two very good reasons. First, you want to learn — whether in a class or on your own — how to play a sport well, and you need clear, easy-to-follow instructions to develop the special skills involved. If you want to be a successful player, this book will be of much help to you.

Second, you may already have developed skill in this activity, but want to improve your performance through assessing your weaknesses and correcting your errors. You want to develop further the skills you have now and to learn and perfect additional ones. You realize that you will enjoy the activity even more if you know more about it.

In either case, this book can contribute greatly to your success. It offers "lessons" from a real professional: from an outstandingly successful coach, teacher, or performer. All the authors in the *Saunders Physical Activities Series* are experts and widely recognized in their specialized fields. Some have been members or coaches of teams of national prominence and Olympic fame.

This book, like the others in our Series, has been written to make it easy for you to help yourself to learn. The author and the editors want you to become more self-motivated and to gain a greater understanding of, appreciation for, and proficiency in the exciting world of *movement*. All the activities described in this Series — sports, games, dance, body conditioning, and weight and figure control activities — require skillful, efficient movement. That's what physical activity is all about. Each book contains descriptions and helpful tips about the nature, value, and purpose of an activity, about the purchase and care of equipment, and about the fundamentals of each movement skill involved. These books also tell you about common errors and how to avoid making them, about ways in which you can improve your performance, and about game rules and strategy, scoring, and special techniques. Above all, they should tell you how to get the most pleasure and benefit from the time you spend.

Our purpose is to make you a successful *participant* in this age of sports activities. If you are successful, you will participate often — and this will give you countless hours of creative and recreative fun. At the same time, you will become more physically fit.

"Physical fitness" is more than just a passing fad or a slogan. It is a condition of your body which determines how effectively you can perform your daily work and play and how well you can meet unexpected demands on your strength, your physical skills, and your endurance. How fit you are depends largely on your participation in vigorous physical activity. Of course no one sports activity can provide the kind of total workout of the body required to achieve optimal fitness; but participation with vigor in any activity makes a significant contribution to this total. Consequently, the activity you will learn through reading this book can be extremely helpful to you in developing and maintaining physical fitness now and throughout the years to come.

These physiological benefits of physical activity are important beyond question. Still, the pure pleasure of participation in physical activity will probably provide your strongest motivation. The activities taught in this Series are *fun,* and they provide a most satisfying kind of recreation for your leisure hours. Also they offer you great personal satisfaction in achieving success in skillful performance — in the realization that you are able to control your body and its movement and to develop its power and beauty. Further, there can be a real sense of fulfillment in besting a skilled opponent or in exceeding a goal you have set for yourself. Even when you fall short of such triumphs, you can still find satisfaction in the effort you have made to meet a challenge. By participating in sports you can gain greater respect for yourself, for others, and for "the rules of the game." Your skills in leadership and fellowship will be sharpened and improved. Last, but hardly least, you will make new friends among others who enjoy sports activities, both as participants and as spectators.

We know you're going to enjoy this book. We hope that it — and the others in our Series — will make you a more skillful and more enthusiastic performer in all the activities you undertake.

Good luck!

MARYHELEN VANNIER
HOLLIS FAIT

CONTENTS

1☐ The Nature of the Game

Someone is bowling every minute in our modern world. Pins are falling, scores are being marked, and centers are crowded with enthusiastic players. Bowling has become an avocation for some participants, a vocation for others, and a fixation to most of those who are actively involved. Those who use it as an avocation may call it recreation, for it can provide relaxation when playing with friends or even alone.

The recreational bowler constitutes the largest part of the estimated 72 million bowlers in America. He often includes his whole family in this activity. Many bowling centers have couple leagues, mother-daughter leagues, and father-son or any other combination of family bowling in sanctioned league competition. The recreational bowler includes every age group from eight to 80. Grandparents are seen teaching their second-generation offspring the game, for bowling does not discriminate against age or those who are handicapped. It is a game that is easily adapted for the blind, the deaf, the mentally retarded, and even those who are crippled and confined to wheel chairs.

The second group, the vocational bowlers, belong to an organization known as the Professional Bowlers' Association. These men and women earn their income by bowling in tournaments, giving demonstrations, making personal appearances, and generally putting bowling before the public eye. They write books and newspaper columns, endorse bowling equipment, and in many cases own their own "bowling palaces." Bowling for the professional becomes a way of life, and since bowling is not seasonal, they often travel extensively all year long. Although their income from tournaments alone cannot match that of the professional basketball or football player, with the fringe benefits of personal appearances and personally autographed equipment, they usually make a good income. The professional performs often as an individual, but he may belong to a league of professionals and thus compete with a team also. Generally, the professional bowls six to 12 games per day in practice or exhibition. Naturally, the more skilled the professional, the greater his income will be.

Bowling is unique in that almost 100 per cent of the people who watch the game also play it. Herein lies the group with a bowling fixation, for the game has

1

gained a hold on these people's lives: as addicted individuals they can be found four to six times weekly on their local lanes. These are the participants who have been bitten by the "bowling bug"; playing the game is no longer recreation to them. The middle age group usually fit into this category if they have been sports enthusiasts all their lives. Bowling is also an ideal game for those who have been retired or are still active oldsters. These are the serious bowlers who do not have either the time or the talent necessary to become professionals. They are the students of the game, they read about it, they go to see the pros in action, and they enter as many local and state tournaments as possible. While most leagues last for nine months, this type of bowler will join a summer league or two to keep his bowling skills polished. Bowling has developed the bowling "widow" just as golf has spawned her Sunday golf counterpart. The bowler in this seriously dedicated group will score just enough high games to keep him coming back.

Television and other communication media have played an important role in acquainting the public with this sport. Local stations often have television tournaments for area bowlers and give prizes as added inducements to watch the programs. The best bowlers in our sports world can be seen regularly through the winter months via the television set. Thus, bowling is out of the centers and into our living rooms with a flip of the switch. The Bowling Proprietors' Association usually sponsors these local shows, and they can be seen live every week from a different lane in a large town or from the same lane in a smaller community.

Bowling is one of the most popular social games in America today. In the sixties, the Lifetime Sports Foundation developed a superior educational and instructional program in bowling as well as golf, badminton, archery, and tennis. Clinics in these sports were conducted periodically by master teachers throughout the nation for both the player and instructor in each of these sports.*

THE PURPOSE OF THE GAME

The game of bowling is a test of precision and accuracy. It is played on a 41½-inch wide alleyway, which is 62 feet, 10¾ inches in length. The object of the game is to knock down the ten pins that stand at the foot of the lane. The body must be so disciplined that it can repeat exactly the smooth pendulum motion necessary for perfect performance. The bowler may have a second chance if he fails to knock down all the pins with the first ball. If he cannot *strike* (clear all the pins with one ball), he then will attempt to *spare* (clear all the remaining pins with the second ball). This effort constitutes the division of scoring called the frame. There are ten frames in a game of bowling and three games to a competitive match. When a bowler throws a perfect game, he has scored 300. This means 12 balls in ten frames. The date a scoring method was

*For further information concerning this program, write to The American Association for Health and Physical Education, 1601 Sixteenth St. N.W., Washington, D.C. 20009.

conceived has not been accurately recorded, but the ten-frame game–three-game match has proved a challenge and a source of satisfaction through the years.

THE HISTORY OF THE GAME

The first historical record of a game similar to bowling came from Egypt. Historians have found pictures on the walls of historic ruins depicting Egyptian men rolling round rocks down an alleyway at rough stonelike objects. There is also a historical record showing that the ancient Polynesians played a game that was a mixture of bowling, hopscotch, and shuffleboard. In this record, it is said that a smooth flat rock was thrown a distance similar to the length of the present alleybed. Bowling was one of man's first forms of recreation, for both these records were made thousands of years before the birth of Christ.

At about the time of Christ, the Romans played a game that had been adapted from their war maneuvers. The Romans did much of their fighting in hilly areas, so one of their tactical maneuvers was to roll rocks down a pass to attract or bowl over the oncoming enemy. The soldiers practiced to develop skill in this tactic and before long began to "play" this game for fun. The Italian sport of bocce originates from this early Roman war game, and the Romans popularized the game as they conquered many nations through Central Europe and villages in England.

The English have written records dating from early in the eleventh century of a game called skittles. The round object was still rolled — but at a tall, thin wooden figurine shaped like a candle with a flat bottom set up in the out-of-doors. This was a popular game with the English peasantry, and it was played with great gusto in their village squares.

While the English were playing this game of skittles, the Germans and Dutch were involved in a strange religious service. These were the Dark Ages in Europe when religion was often an oppression rather than a comfort. The heide (later called kegle) was a rounded wooden object with a flat bottom that stood about 2 feet tall at the end of the church altar and represented man's sins. The worshipper walked into the church, picked a ball-like stone, and rolled it down the aisle toward the heide. If all the heides were knocked down, the sinner had attained atonement. If not, he had to continue with other penances.

People began to practice kegle-throwing away from the church, and rapidly the service changed into a game called kegling. Martin Luther, an early religious figure, enjoyed the game with his fellow countrymen and wrote a set of rules for this game, which he entitled "nine pins." It was played on the grassy commons in the towns and villages and was so popular that it became a major social event in the many small towns.

In the seventeenth century the English, Dutch, and Germans began to immigrate to the New World, bringing the game of nine pins with them. The common Dutch displayed the greatest interest, and so the people of New Amsterdam (New York) played this in their New World home. In both England and the

Colonies, the game became so popular that players began to gain considerable skill. Because of this skill the players began to bet on their own ability and observers on their favorite player. Gambling progressed to the point that the English Parliament eventually outlawed the game of nine pins. Then some colonist with ingenuity added another pin to the game. The name of the game was changed to Bowls and it flourished again. The gambling decreased as the popularity of the game flourished.

The Southern Colonies had a game called duck pins, played with a small ball and a short, squatty pin. The game was played indoors in the South and was the most popular of all the bowling-type games there until after the 1950's. When alleys were first built in the southern United States, three-fourths of the lanes were constructed for duck pins. The coastal states played a game called candlesticks with pins that were taller and thinner. The ball was still held in the palm of the hand, and the game was a close cousin to the English game of skittles.

In the 1800's the game of bowls was refined and indoor bowling alleys were built. One of the first indoor alleys was on Manhattan Island. The game moved west but was played for the most part on a green grassy strip. The term "bowling on the green," was a common one, and many towns derived their name from the game. Bowling Green is now a common name for a city or town in the states that had German or Dutch settlers. Gradually other changes came about; the ball was drilled with two finger holes and was increased in size. The game began to have standardized rules, and with this standardization a structured game with specific rules developed.*

Until the early 1900's the game was played almost exclusively by men. In the 1890's a group known as the American Bowling Congress (ABC) was formed. This organization set up rules, tournaments, and awards for all-male bowlers. Most of the alleys were centered in large towns and located north and east of the Mississippi River. New York, Buffalo, Cleveland, Chicago, and Cincinnati became the centers of these bowling activities.

In the early 1900's women began to assert their independence, and in 1916 a small group of women organized the Women's International Bowling Congress. The bowling alley of the day was an unsavory place. Women really had no place in this environment, for the early alleys were connected with the local tavern, saloon, or pool hall where men went to talk and be with other men to play cards or bowl a game or two.

The Second World War brought women into bowling alleys in increasing numbers. At that time 50 per cent of the young men were fighting abroad, and the young women had taken over the jobs in the factories and war plants. They often had free time on their hands after working hours. Industrial leaders realized that these women needed to find recreational outlets in order to increase both their health and their productivity, so they built bowling alleys near industrial centers. Bowling alley owners set up leagues for the factory workers, and often

---

*In 1875, the National Bowling Association unified the widely diverse rules, but then quickly gave way to the ABC.

alleys were open 24 hours around the clock. When a bowler came off her shift job, she would join friends in a competitive industrial league game, as did male factory workers not engaged in the armed forces.

Because of the large numbers of women coming to the alleys, the environment of the alleys began to change and became more of a family center. Women from all economic levels flocked to these bowling houses. Today the number of females involved in the competitive bowling program is about 500 per cent greater than what it was 25 years ago, and the growth of women participants as compared to men in competitive bowling in the last decade has been about four to one. In 1916 there were 40 women members of the WIBC; today there are 4.2 million female members. As the number of bowlers of both sexes has increased in the past 25 years, so also has their degree of skill improved. Averages are 30 pins higher than they were in the 1940's when bowling began to boom and become a business and a popular recreational outlet for people of all ages.

In 1943, the National Bowling Council was formed to coordinate all bowling information and education, and it remains today as a clearing-house for bowling materials. Alberta Crowe of New York has been a strong, steady worker for the women's bowling movement. She served 25 years as president of the WIBC and currently serves as President of the National Bowling Council.

The Bowling Hall of Fame is now under construction in St. Louis, Mo. This tribute will house bowling's history.

2□Facilities, Equipment, and Their Care

A person who is interested in experimenting with the game of bowling can easily do so without purchasing any equipment. All bowling establishments provide house balls of different sizes, and shoes are rented for a nominal fee as a public relations device to get the novice started in this sport. In many bowling centers a bowling instructor is available at certain times of the day to aid the new bowler. The instructor may be a local professional and might be compared to the pro at a city golf course who gives lessons. Many times bowlers in leagues may consult the professional in their "house" when they have been having a slump in their game.

THE HOUSE

Most modern bowling houses, or leisure centers as they are frequently called, are in low buildings with plenty of parking on the outside. They generally are found in the business or shopping centers of a community and are easily accessible and "where the action is." Most houses are a part of a business syndicate or have been owned for many years by the same family. The construction and operation of a bowling center is expensive. Many lanes have a restaurant, grill, or bar attached as part of the services provided their customers. The lanes of today are beautifully carpeted, soundproofed, and air conditioned. Everything is inside the lanes and is geared to make the customer as comfortable as possible. Today's leisure centers are a far cry from the pool hall saloon and sawdust on the floor of yesteryear. The proprietors now attempt to keep the family customer and the young people who are spending so much of the recreational dollar topmost in their business minds. Some lanes, especially in smaller communities, are still connected with the billiard or poolrooms. Usually these lanes are the sole recreational facility for a small community. In the larger cities, a bowling center with only 12 lanes is considered a small establishment. Most modern houses provide 24 to 48 lanes for their bowling public.

The lanes are usually completely taken over nightly by bowling leagues. Most lanes operate two shifts per evening, but in areas where there is heavy factory participation, the bowler may have the opportunity to bowl a "night owl" shift starting at 12 or 1 in the morning. During the day, leagues are in full swing, and many proprietors provide another public relations service, the day nursery.

When school is out, students take over and bowl in the American Junior Bowling Congress* leagues run by the bowling proprietor or by an interested teacher in the school's intramural program. Most bowling centers are happy to cooperate with the school, and many give cut-rate prices to encourage the school after-class programs. Some lanes are in close proximity to the school and can offer a facility for the regular physical education classes.

The student unions of most universities now have a dozen or so lanes to accommodate their bowling community. These lanes are a part of the recreational center, and most game room managers sponsor college leagues for students, staff, and the faculty. During the day most of the lanes are turned into an educational center for the physical education classes. Bowling is often the most elected of physical education activities in the college curriculum, possibly because 't is a game that is relatively easy to learn and one doesn't have to change clothing to play it. It could also be because of its great carry-over into later life.

PIN SETTING MACHINES

The largest and most expensive single piece of equipment in the lanes is the pin setting machine. This, like most machines, has run the gamut of modernization techniques. Like so many others, this business has tried to keep up with the demands for speed and ease of operation.

Hand Setting Machines

The pin machines were operated until the mid-1950's by boys who picked the pins off the deck and out of the pit and put them onto a table. The pinboy then lowered the machine to the pin deck and the pins stood in place. The boy had to be constantly on his toes or the bowler would complain about his lack of speed in returning the ball or resetting the pins. There was always the chance too that a bowler might bowl a second ball before the pinboy had gotten out of the pit. The boys soon invented a system of first setting the pins and then returning the bowler's ball. Complete mechanization moved into the bowling alleys in the

---

*The American Junior Bowling Congress has merged with the Youth Bowling Association to become the Young American Bowling Alliance as of August 1, 1982.

1950's and the often-berated boys were removed from the pits. The pinboy of old has been replaced by a rapidly functioning piece of modern machinery. Many present professional bowlers got their first taste of the game at the other end of the lane as a youngster.

Automatic Pin Setters

Present-day pin setters are electronic machines that operate without human prompting. When a ball hits the cushion at the rear of the pit, the pin sweeper is activated and drops slowly to the deck. The table then comes down and picks up the remaining pins. The sweeper moves backward and clears the fallen pins (dead wood) into a belt in the pit. The table returns the leave to the pin deck for the bowler to shoot the spare. The ball is carried to and through the ball return by the belt while the pins are carried around the side and up into the rack again. The front panel lights automatically, showing the bowler which pins must be shot for the spare conversion. If the bowler knocks down all the pins on the first ball (strike), the front panel will light up a large X or a crown.

There are several companies that manufacture this expensive piece of equipment. The cost of one automatic electronic pin setting device is close to $10,000. The companies that sell this equipment also train technicians for its care and repair. Most centers have at least two men who have been to electronic pin setting schools, and they are on duty at all times in case of breakdown or malfunction. The automatic machines are cleaned and oiled almost daily to insure their continued performance.

As IBM machines are programmed to do special jobs, the automatic pin setter has two other programmings from which it can operate. The first of these is the shadow ball set-up. The shadow ball is thrown by the teams before the match to enable them to study and judge the conditions of the alley. The machine, in this instance, does not set or clear pins; its function is only to return the ball to the rack. The bowler throws only at shadows or imagined pin set-ups. The second of the programmings is the headpin tournament set-up. In this mechanical process the automatic pin setter returns a full deck of pins after a single throw. Thus the bowler rolls 12 times at a full set of pins to complete one game.

PINS

Pin weights may vary as much as 12 ounces, but each set must contain ten pins of like weight with a variation of only 4 ounces. This is why the action from the pins due to weight varies from alley to alley. The action of one pin against another is an important factor in gaining the strike. Some types of deliveries cause the pins to mix more than others. Probably the best mixing ball is the curve, because the spinning ball causes the pins to react against each other. The lighter the pin, the faster the pins will fly on a pocket hit, but this may also be all in a backward direction depending upon how much force was imparted by

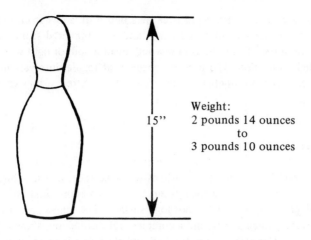

15"   Weight:
          2 pounds 14 ounces
                    to
          3 pounds 10 ounces

the bowler. A good bowler learns after a few practice tries (shadow balls) how the ball is working. Certain centers gain the reputation for having live pins and high scoring lanes because of the maintenance care given the lanes and pins by the proprietor.

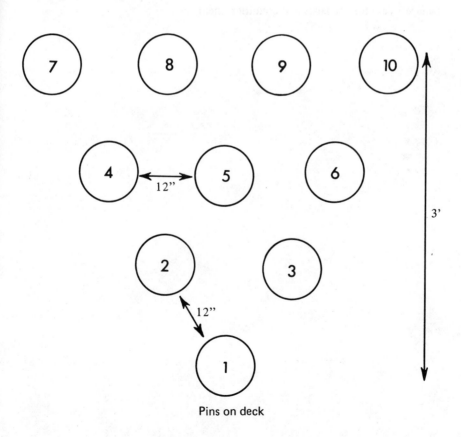

Pins on deck

The pins are set up on the pin deck at a depth of 3 feet from the pit. They are set up in four rows forming a triangle and are numbered from left to right. They are sometimes referred to as new wood, dead wood, or light wood, depending upon their condition. The pins are checked at regular intervals and replaced whenever necessary. Competitive pins are white with red stripes encircling the neck of the pin.

THE LANE

The lane bed is constructed of a hard wood surface, which is highly waxed and glossy. The hard wood surface is put together in approximately 1-inch-wide strips fitted perfectly into a 63-foot-long surface. The alleys are stripped of all wax and surfacing once a year, and a complete refinishing job is done. Lanes that are heavily waxed or sticky slow the ball and thus give it more chance for rotation and a wide arc. Those that are buffed and running fast will not give the ball a chance to break into the pins, causing the ball to travel three-fourths of the way down the lane before it begins to turn. The bowler must learn to "read" his lane while practicing so that he can either throw harder in the case of a slow lane or ease up for a fast lane. Much of bowling success depends upon the way center managers care for the lanes and condition them.

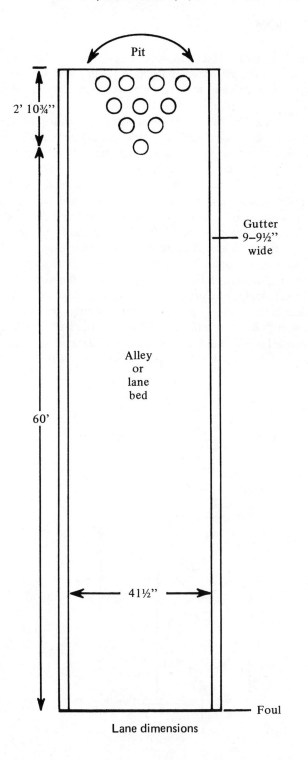

Lane dimensions

BALL RETURNS

Most bowling centers built now have returns that are built under the floor and run parallel to the gutter separating each set of lanes. They usually can be reached from above the floor by lifting a wood panel. Balls do occasionally get caught in this chute, especially the lighter ball that does not return with enough speed. In older houses the balls come down a chute from the pit and are returned above the floor to the ball rack. The ball rack comes in several structural forms.

Straight racks were the earliest type of return. They ran the entire length of the approach and were the end of the above-floor return. They have been abandoned in the most modern lanes, because they seem to hinder the bowler's concentration and do not allow enough room for body movement or "english." Also a part of the early straight rack were the chalk ball and common towel. The bowler would use the chalk instead of air to keep his hands dry and keep the ball from slipping off his fingers. Both these devices were thought unsanitary and were removed from the lanes. The bowlers often would chalk the soles of their shoes, and this would present another problem of maintenance.

The T-rack is still a part of many lanes. It was adopted because the length could be shortened so that it became less of a distraction to the bowler. The problem here is that many times the ball was on the lane opposite the bowler who was approaching for the first ball in a frame. Because of this inconvenience the manufacturers began to look for a new, more convenient set-up.

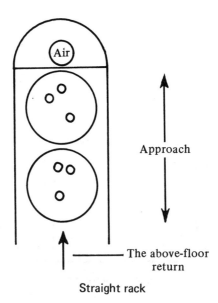

Straight rack

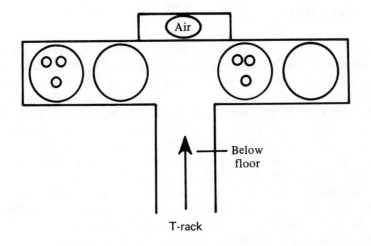

T-rack

The most modern rack is round with a swivel plate in the center. The bowler turns the plate and picks up the ball with less effort. The return is very close to the end of the approach and so insures the least distraction. The bowling industry has made bowling popular because, among other things, its efforts increasingly make bowling fun and seemingly effortless.

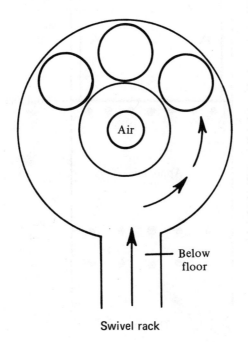

Swivel rack

THE APPROACH

The approach is a softer wood than that of the alley bed, so that when a ball is dropped behind the foul line it seems to lose some of its roll and lands with a dead sound. The length of the approach is 15 feet, and a bowler may start from any point behind the foul line and within the approach area. The approach is marked with a set of dots immediately at the foul line and a set 12 feet back toward the scoring table. These dots give the bowler an idea of where he starts and finishes within his walking approach. Fifteen feet down the alley from the foul line are some arrow-like figures called spots or marks. There is a point on these spots over which the ball should cross in order to record a strike. This point is not the same for every bowler, so it is necessary for the bowler to experiment until he finds "his spot." These points of concentration were placed on the alley to aid the bowler visually and cut down on distractive elements.

The foul line is electronically lit so that if a bowler crosses the beam of light, a bell rings on the lane. The bowler has fouled because he has broken the ray of light. Sometimes a person is able to avoid the beam, but if any part of the body

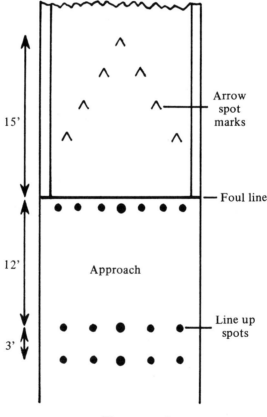

The approach

has touched the lane beyond the foul line, he is considered as having committed the foul and the score he has made is not counted.

SCORING DEVICES

The most commonly used scoring device is the score sheet upon which the frames are printed. The bowlers take turns marking score for each other. The modern lane has also adopted the overhead projector method of marking. A crayon and a clear plastic, preprinted transparency are used. The scores are shown on the projector, and everyone at the rear of the lanes can see how the bowler is progressing. These are used for league play only and can be cleaned and reused.

An innovation is the automatic scoring machine, which works electronically. After the bowler throws, the pins are reset and the score is automatically tallied. The part of the machine that is attached to the ball return looks somewhat like a computer system. Only the final pin total registers. Each bowler's name is inserted into a slot numbered 1 through 5 on a single side of the machine. The automatic scorer keeps count for all ten bowlers in a match.*

PERSONAL EQUIPMENT

Selecting a Ball

The weight of a ball varies from 8 to 16 pounds. Some smaller women use the 9 or 10 pound balls because of their lack of strength. The 8, 9, and 10 pound balls are manufactured mainly for the physically handicapped and young people who have not developed full strength. Most centers have a wide selection of the light balls to accommodate those not wanting to purchase their own ball.†

More important than the weight of the ball is getting a span that fits the bowler's hand comfortably. The thumb hole should be large enough that the ball will not stick to the thumb but should fit closely so that the bowler can grip on the lift. If the bowler has to grip too tightly because of the oversize thumb hole, blisters soon develop from the constant pressure and scraping of the ball.

The two center fingers should feel as comfortable in the ball as the thumb. Some bowlers feel more at ease with the fingers inserted up to the second knuckle. This is the conventional grip and is the type used by the novices when selecting a lane or house ball. When the ball is resting in the hand, the palm

---

*Bowling proprietors are finding that it takes a lot of their time to teach the use of computer scoring. This may run the route of modern math because many players find it confusing and prefer keeping score.

†Bowlers intending to bowl weekly should be fit for their own balls by a reputable dealer. This is the best way to gain consistency and comfort.

Conventional grip

should be fairly flat against the ball surface. The skin between the thumb and the first finger should not be uncomfortably stretched or taut. A correctly fitting ball is necessary for consistent ball delivery.

The semi-grip ball is held with the two center fingers inserted to between the first and second knuckle. Men sometimes use this grip to alleviate the tendency to hold onto the ball too long.

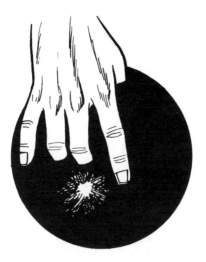

Semi-grip

Finger-tip grip

The third grip choice is the finger-tip hold. This grip is effected by the use of the ends of the two fingers and insures quick release of the ball. This grip may also make possible a larger arc in the bowler's delivery; many men who wish to get more spin on their delivery will use this particular grip. Most women do not select the semi-grip or the finger-tip grip because of their small finger size and lack of strength.

Balls are now sold in many colors and patterns, designed to appeal to the female bowling market. Most are made of a hard rubber composition, but a new plastic product is also available. A bowler may use the same ball for 10 to 20 years and then sometimes will change only because of ebbing strength or altered hand size. A good ball costs upwards of 35 dollars.

Dress

The most important part of the needed apparel is the shoe. Shoes should fit comfortably, but this does not mean that they must be unstylish. Again, women have played a large part in getting the manufacturers to produce more appealing street-like styles. The right-handed bowler should always have a leather sole on the left shoe or the sliding foot and a rubber sole on the right shoe.* If the bowler is left-handed, the soles are reversed. Most men wear a pair of slacks and a short-sleeved sport shirt for bowling. Women have broken the traditional dress

---

*There is also a new shoe with a composition sole and no need for a difference in the right/left shoe.

patterns and wear the sports clothes popular today. Men continue to set the pace in the purchase of equipment, many times carrying two balls to deal with varying lane conditions.

Bowling Gadgets

Some bowlers may wear a bowling glove on the bowling hand to stop perspiration and to give the ball firm support. Many women wear an elastic or leather wrist band to give added support and to remind them to hold the wrist firm while the ball is released. Most bowlers use either a towel or a small rosin bag to keep the hands free of moisture.

3 □ The Mechanics of Bowling

The bowler approaches the ball rack and picks up the ball with both hands. The hands should approach the sides of the ball so that the fingers are not crushed when the balls hit together as they are returned. The bowler should never pick up the ball with his fingers in the holes. Since the fingers have a tendency to perspire, it is best not to grip the ball too tightly until just before the pendulum motion begins. Then, too, the bowler who lacks finger strength will also tire more easily because of the constant hoisting of the heavy ball with his fingers.

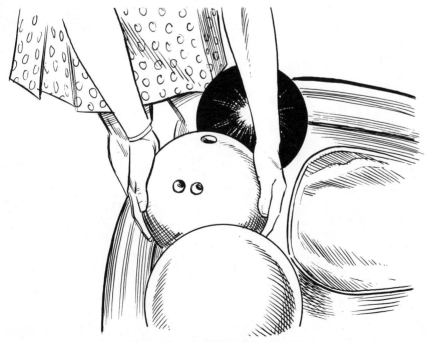

Correct way to lift ball from rack

The bowler approaches the lane with the ball held in both hands; the stance is taken in preparation to rolling the ball. The feet are lined up with the dots approximately 12 feet back from the foul line. The distance from the foul line varies with each bowler, for the length of the stride determines how far back from the foul line the bowler must stand. The positioning of the feet, other than the distance from the foul line, will be discussed with each of the individual types of delivery. Approaches in different bowling centers are standard so the bowler can always identify his starting position.

The beginning bowler is most comfortable when standing in a comfortable erect position. The line of gravity should run straight up the side of the body with the weight centered over the base of the body (the feet). The feet are slightly apart, increasing the size of the base and thus effecting the better balance.

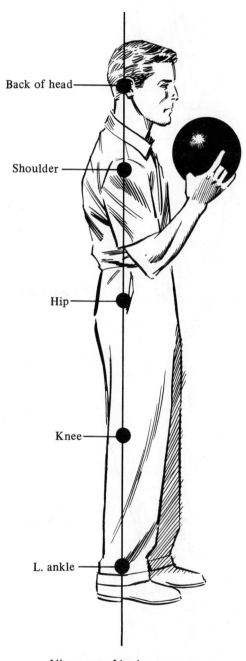

Back of head

Shoulder

Hip

Knee

L. ankle

Alignment of body at stance

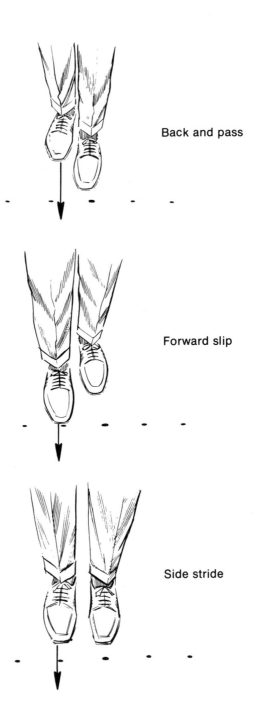

Back and pass

Forward slip

Side stride

STANCE POSITIONS OF THE FEET

The feet may start in any of three positions. The back and pass position is generally recommended, because it is the natural stride position with the right leg passing the left. In this position most of the weight is on the forward foot. In the forward slip position the right foot is forward. Most of the weight is still on the left foot; the right foot in this stance slides forward in a short motion. The third position is the side stride, and it is not generally recommended because the beginner has a tendency to roll the weight of his body back on the heels. Either of the first two positions is acceptable; the bowler decides which affords him easy coordination.

STANCE POSITIONS OF THE BALL

The beginning bowler should face the pins squarely. It is only in more advanced techniques that a person should or would have any other starting position. The bowler should begin and finish on the approach with his shoulders squarely facing the pins. The ball may be held close to the body in one of three positions. The most consistent of these is the ball at waist position, and this is recommended for the novice bowler. In second position the ball is held between the waist and the knee. This is not the best position, especially for a person of short stature because it cuts down on the length of the pendulum swing. Also, the body weight is forward, and this may cause running or rushing of the foul line. In the third starting position the ball is almost at shoulder height with the bowler looking over the top of the ball. This position will find the bowler using up part of the third step in getting the ball down to his side; thus the back-swing is shortened to compensate for the delayed backward motion. In any of the three cases the ball is supported with both hands in the stance position. It is recommended that the ball usually be held slightly to the right of the midline of the body. The bowler should be relaxed and concentrate upon doing each movement accurately.

The point of concentration is taken with the eyes and mind as the bowler puts his fingers into the ball. At this point the bowler is ready to begin forward motion. The span of pose before beginning should not be too long, because the bowler's hands will begin to perspire quickly and on the release the ball will slip prematurely from the fingers. By the same token the forward motion should not come as if the bowler were being shot from a cannon, because the pause before the approach is the moment of concentration.

THE APPROACH

The approach is the bowler's means of moving to the foul line to deliver the ball. Most experts agree that there are three approaches possible — the three,

Waist ball

Above head

Ball at knee

four, and five step approaches. The number of professional bowlers using the three step approach is almost negligible. Because these knowledgeable and skilled individuals are eliminating this technique, this book will also eliminate a description of the mechanics of the three step approach for the beginner. The reason for not teaching the three step approach is fairly evident. First, three steps do not allow enough time for a finished pendulum arm motion; the bowler either eliminates his push forward or cuts down on the back swing. Second, those persons who use three steps have a tendency to rush the foul line and take steps that are abnormally long. The other two approaches are what professional bowlers call good legitimate approaches. The following approaches are discussed for the *right-handed* bowler.

The Four Step Approach

The footwork in the approach is claimed by some bowling instructors to be the most important part of the mechanics of bowling. It is important for the bowler to start slowly and to accelerate as he reaches the second, third, and fourth steps. Coordination of hand and foot must be practiced constantly in order that the bowler may achieve timing consistency for accurate delivery.

The first step of this approach is a short step with the right foot pointing straight ahead. Some professional bowlers call the first step a shuffle step. It is a brief sliding step forward by the right foot. The second and third steps are fairly evenly spaced and in the same rhythm. The last step is a slide and is longer than the second or third step. Again, the toe of the left foot is pointing straight ahead. The sliding foot should finish within 6 inches of the foul line.

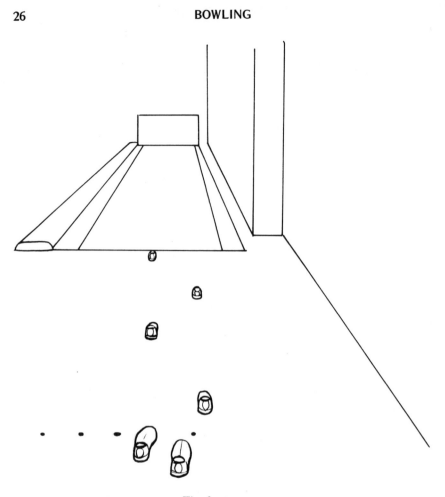

The foot pattern

Pendulum arm motion

First Step. The arms with the ball held in both hands push forward (extend) to a point no farther out than the right foot is forward. The motion is called the "pushaway." The arms should never extend fully because the person will be pulled off balance.

Second Step. On the second step the left hand releases the ball and begins to act as an aid in balance. The right hand drops the ball to a position at the side of the right leg and close to the body. It is important at this point that the wrist be firm and straight.

Third Step. The body is leaning forward and the knees are slightly bent in this step, causing an acceleration of body movement. The arm is drawn straight back with the fingers gripping firmly. At the completion of this step the ball

The pushaway

Downward

Backward arm swing

reaches its highest point in the back swing. This point should be no higher than the shoulders and no lower than the waist for best control and application of force.

Fourth Step. As the left foot starts forward, the right arm comes forward in a straight line with a firm wrist. As the slide begins, the arm passes the right side of the body. The ball swings out and upward toward the pins as the slide is completed, with the fingers releasing the ball at this moment. The weight of the ball and gravity aid the bowler in swinging the ball forward. If the ball is carried or directed forward, some of the lift is lost and the bowler has a tendency to hold the ball too long. The weight is on the ball of the foot until the point of release is reached wherein the heel of the foot comes down to aid the bowler's balance. The legs are bent and the body is leaning forward, the eyes and head focusing on the spot. The ball is released by the thumb first; the fingers then give the ball the last-moment roll (explosion), which aids in an active pin splash. The ball should contact the floor beyond the foul line for best roll. This does not mean it is lofted out onto the playing surface like a softball, but it is *rolled* on the release onto the lane bed. The teacher of bowling should refrain from using "throw" or "toss" or "lift" or "put" in place of the word "roll-ll-ll-ll." That term defines clearly the physical action desired at point of release.

Forward arm swing

Follow through

This is the point at which many bowlers fail on the approach. Once the ball is released, they drop their arm and turn from the pins. Bowlers should be interested in what their ball is going to do, and so it is advisable to continue to face the pins squarely until they fall. The arm should continue its upward motion and finish in an arc close to the top of the head. Some instructors tell the beginner to bring his hand up to his nose. The finish of the arm swing is important to the completion of an action roll. The beginning bowler should check the position of his left foot at the foul line upon completion of the delivery. The position of the feet may be a clue to the direction the bowler was facing on the release or whether he had walked a straight path toward the pins.

THE FIVE STEP APPROACH

The five step approach is used primarily by people who cannot retrain their sidedness. Even when a bowler is right-handed, he may have a tendency to start all his motions with the left side of his body. He probably was forced into the use of his right hand at an early age, although his brain was programmed from birth for left-sidedness. It is simpler for this person to start his approach on the left foot forward step. This preliminary step is actually a mock step, a very short

Completion of arm swing

shuffle. Sometimes it is nothing more than an exchange of weight from the left foot to the right foot. Some people prefer the shortened steps of this approach to the gliding steps of the four step approach. Observers may say that this five step bowler looks as if he is tiptoeing toward or sneaking up on the foul line. Many times in this approach the heel does not touch the floor on the first two steps.

The pushaway does not start until the beginning of the second step. The second step increases somewhat in length, and the pushaway motion of the arms is no longer than in the four step approach. The third and fourth steps are similar to those of the four step approach, with the arm dropping down and backward. The slide finds the arm coming through to the point of release.

A few bowlers pushaway on the first step, but they then must compensate by increasing the height of the backswing. Three steps are taken when the ball is dropping down and back instead of the usual two steps. It is an altogether different kind of coordination than is required by any other approach.

All human beings have a unique physical movement appearance, almost like their hand print. This movement rhythm causes each person to look different as he makes his bowling approach. There is no robot look we can impose upon the beginner that is best for him. There are just the basic suggestions which a beginner uses as a guide.

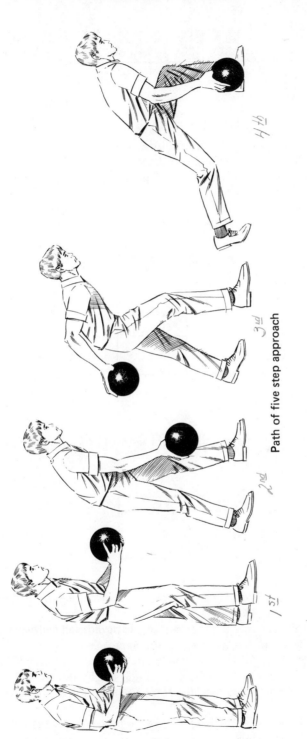

Path of five step approach

4th

3rd

2nd

1st

5 step

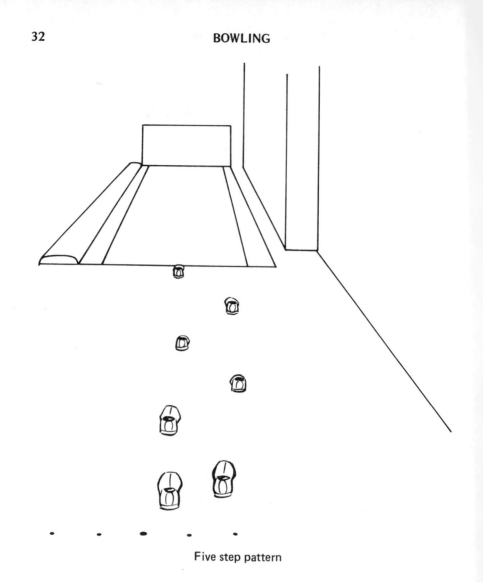

Five step pattern

THE DELIVERY

The action of the ball in delivery is a result of the path the ball takes in going down the lane bed. This path is a product of the type of grip the bowler employs upon the ball. The action of delivery begins with the grip at the stance and continues through all arm motions in the approach and release. There are four methods of delivery. Three methods are considered best and are used most often. The fourth type of delivery is a result of physical structure or handicap. The four types of delivery are the hook, the straight ball, the reverse hook, and the curve.

The hook is by far the best delivery for attaining the strike, for the amount of pin action or splash is probably twice that of the straight ball. The straight ball is for the once-a-week bowler who enjoys a controlled or spare delivery. It is very doubtful that anyone uses a true straight ball delivery — the ball in most cases tails off or breaks in at some point on the lane. The reverse hook or back-up ball is thought by most bowlers to be an error, but with the increased number of women bowling who have weaker wrists than men, this delivery is being accepted by bowling instructors as one of the legitimate means of rolling the ball. The instructor working with a bowler who has developed a reverse delivery will work to give this individual the best method of rolling this delivery. A right-handed bowler should begin his approach as if he were a left-handed bowler, that is, as if he were about to roll the ball in the 1-2 pocket. (Some women's inability to throw a softball correctly is a result, incidentally, of the same splayed elbow and tight shoulder musculature which make certain methods of delivery less effective for them than others.) The curve, the fourth delivery discussed, is an effective strike ball, but is often very difficult to control when attempting a spare conversion.

The Hook

Depending upon the size of the hook, the path of the ball is from the right side in toward the three pin. About three-fourths of the way down the lane, the ball breaks to the left and in toward the headpin. The ball is moving in toward the headpin, and this breaking action imparts the spin or english that bowls over the pins.

The bowler starts and finishes at the right side of the large center dot on the approach. The feet are slightly apart and in the back-and-pass position discussed earlier. Generally the hook bowler walks in a fairly straight line from his stance to his slide at the foul line. The starting position will vary with the condition of the lanes and the arc of the hook.

The hook is the method of delivery chosen by 90 per cent of the professional bowlers. Most instructors start a beginner bowler with the hook hand grip. The hand is placed in the ball with the thumb at the 10 o'clock position. There is a spread V formed by the fingers and the thumb. As the ball is released, the angle of the V is decreased. The open end of the V starts and finishes facing the pins. The fingers are on the side and slightly under the ball, providing support and lift. The wrist is straight and firm above the ball on the forward swing with the arm extended in full range for a large pendulum motion. The thumb leaves the ball first; then the fingers impart the lift that gives the spin or action.

If the beginner bowler aspires to be a "good" bowler or even a professional one day, he must master the hook ball delivery.

Note to Teachers:

Every bowler should be thought of as a possible champion — teach them the champion's techniques!

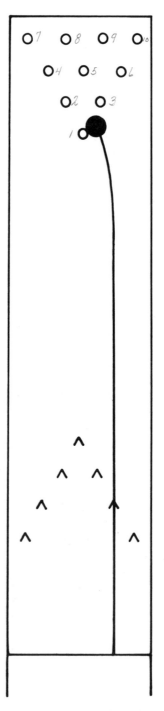

Path of the hook

Position of feet in stance

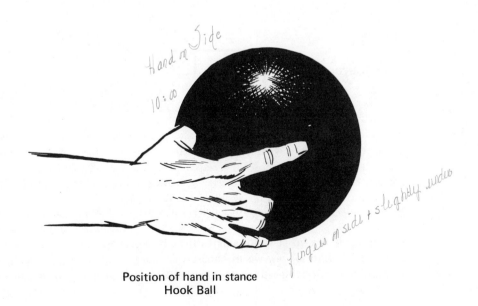

Position of hand in stance
Hook Ball

Position of hand at point of hook release

The Straight Ball

The straight ball is best thrown from the corner in. The bowler starts in approximately the same position as the hook bowler. The ball is released 3 or 4 inches in from the right-hand corner of the lane and should proceed in a direct line to the 1-3 pocket. It is best that the ball hit higher on the 1 than on the 3 to insure carrying the five pin. If the headpin is hit lightly, the ball may be deflected and the five pin will stand. The straight ball thrower may find a lot of 5-7 or 5-10 splits coming up if he throws the light pocket hit.

The straight ball does not present the problem of figuring out how fast or how slow the lanes are running. The fingers are placed in the ball with the thumb at 12 o'clock and the right hand under the ball. The left hand acts as a stabilizer with only a small amount of the ball weight resting on this hand. The ball is released first by the thumb, which is pointing directly upward. The fingers then lift the ball out and upward over the foul line. The palm of the hand is facing

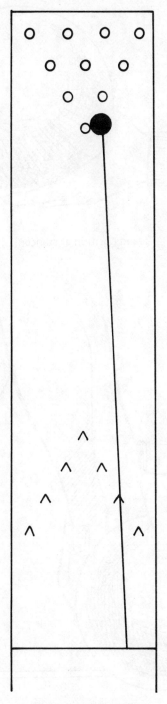

Path of straight ball

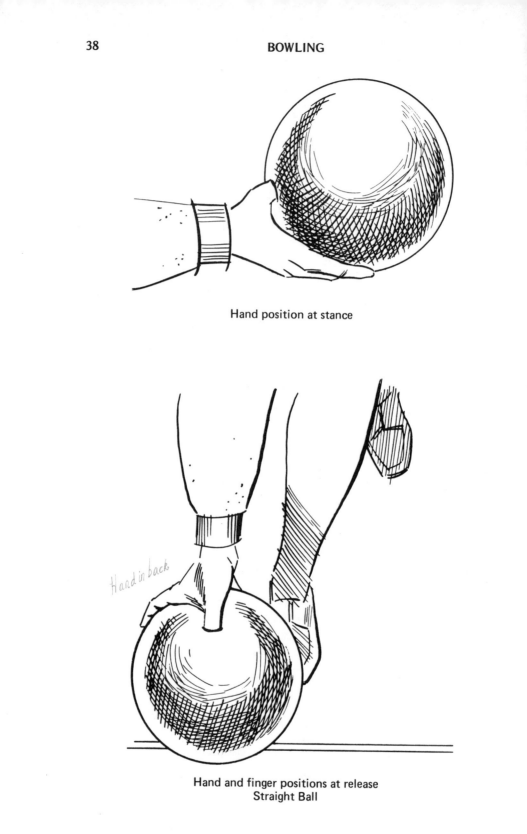

Hand position at stance

Hand in back

Hand and finger positions at release
Straight Ball

the pins at the point of release. The wrist must be just as straight and firm in this delivery as in the hook delivery. No spin or twist is put on the ball; the bowler simply attempts to keep the hand straight in release and follow through. The hand follows through above the head; a good reminder is, if you can, to pat yourself with a flat palm on top of the head.

The Reverse Hook

This delivery has been considered an error by many. The bowler turns his hand away from the line of the roll. Probably the greatest error in this method is that most reverse hook bowlers continue to roll at the 1-3 pocket for a strike. The 1-2 pocket is actually the better pocket for strikes by the reverse hook delivery. When using the pocket on the 1-3 side, the bowler finds the ball backing away from the headpin as it hits the pins. The result is a considerable number of five pins standing instead of attaining the desired strike. When the reverse hook delivery goes into the 1-2 pocket correctly, the ball then backs into the five pin, and we have a delivery as effective as the conventional hook. The ball can be rolled from the left side of the approach or across the body from the right side of the approach. The choice is a matter of comfort and effectiveness. Persons studying body mechanics have begun to know that effective results with low body stress are the best measure of a successful physical performance. Sports such as gymnastics and diving require exactness of body positioning; others allow more individual "body-printing."

The ball rolled from the left side of the lane tracks toward the third range finder from the left.* The object is to hit the 1-2 pocket with a solid exploding roll. The position of the ball during the stance is the same, with the thumb at 12 o'clock, but the positions of the hand are different at release. The hand opens up and the thumb releases toward 2 o'clock. The arm rotates outward from the elbow and away from the midline of the body on the follow through. Many women are using this method of delivery with great effectiveness. The break in the delivery is from left to right and causes a similar spin or splash to result from the turning ball. Although a woman can average 150 to 170 with this delivery, it is not recommended as the best delivery for strikes. Because the ball is being thrown away from the midline of the body, this delivery creates a strain on the human structure. Physical action that is toward the midline of the body is more controlled, especially when weight is involved. Women are not alone in the use of this delivery; some men are now throwing a deceptive reverse hook. They throw the ball hard from the right corner and it is just at the last moment that the ball reverses.

---

*The ball rolled from the right side tracks toward the third or fourth range finder from the right.

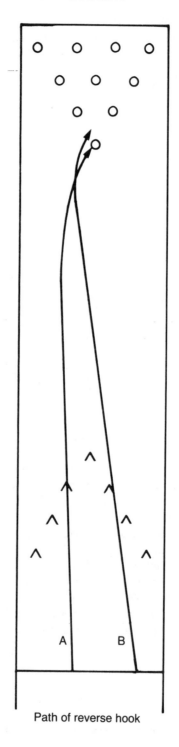

Path of reverse hook

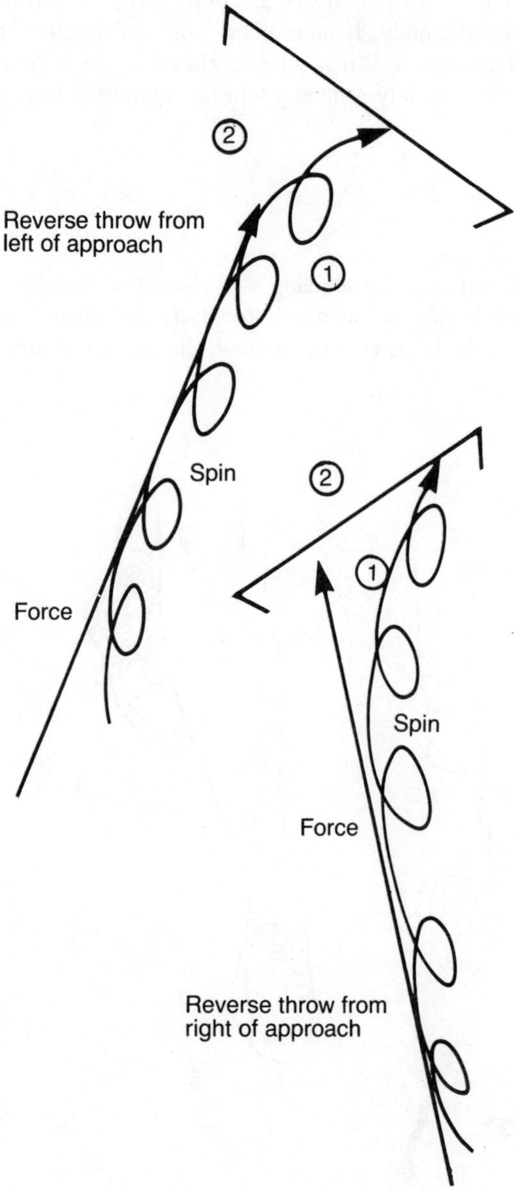

②

Reverse throw from
left of approach

①

Spin   ②

①

Force

Spin

Force

Reverse throw from
right of approach

The bone structure of a woman's arm is different from that of a man's. The woman's elbow has a splayed bone formation, and if the muscles around the elbow joint have not been strengthened and developed, the arm swings naturally away and out from the body. It takes many hours of practice and building of strength for the individual to throw a hook. However, the individual interested in bowling for recreation only generally will not spend the time to develop the better movement.

The Curve

The curve ball can vary considerably with the surface conditions of the lane. When the lanes are highly polished and run fast, the curve ball is truer to its intended arc. When the lanes are dry or slow, the arc of the curve ball increases

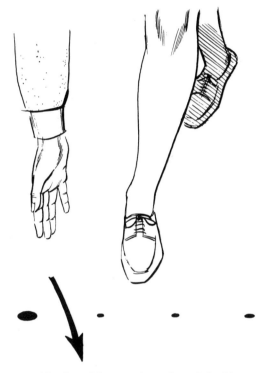

Hand position at release from left side

Hand position on follow through for reverse hook

and the ball becomes very difficult to control. The arc of the ball is from right to left and begins immediately upon release. The beginning stance for the curve may find the right shoulder back from the pins slightly to allow the body a larger movement range on the backswing. The thumb comes out of the hole first, and then the fingers rotate upward to give lift and spin at the point of release.

The ball is held so that the top of the V is facing the pins. The thumb is at the 11 o'clock position and the wrist is cupped so that the fingers are at the side and under the ball. The feet start at the center or slightly to the left of the large center stance dot. The bowler again should walk a fairly straight line and release the ball at almost midpoint of the foul line. The hand in this delivery turns the ball just after the ball passes the side of the body on the forward swing. This is a very difficult maneuver to accomplish with any degree of sameness from time to time. The lack of consistent arc would make this a frustrating delivery for the beginning bowler.

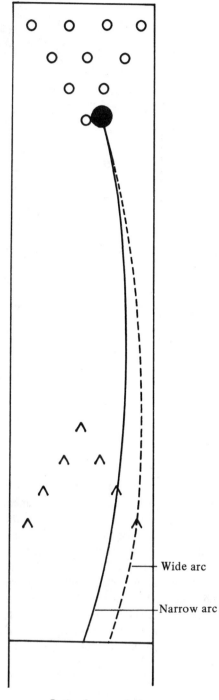

Path of curve delivery

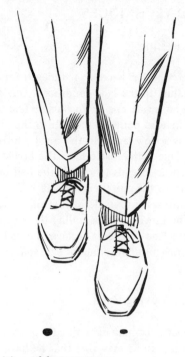

Position of feet at stance

Position of hand at stance
Curve Delivery

ADVANCED TECHNIQUES

Inside-Outside Line

The bowler who has become a student of the game will move around on the approach to adjust to the lane conditions. One of the more skilled techniques is that of rolling an inside line or an outside line. The line in this case is a straight line from the release point of the ball to the pin. If the ball hooks easily on a lane, the lane is a slow lane and the bowler moves accordingly. The best line to roll on a slow lane is the inside line. The bowler moves to the left or inside the spot over which he intends to roll. If the ball breaks only at the last minute or fails to come in to the pin, the alley is fast. The bowler moves a board or two to the right and throws an outside line. (Lane conditions are discussed at length in Chapter 2.) The bowler who is rolling the straight ball does not have to worry too much about lane problems because the ball is rolling only toward the pins; all other deliveries must worry about side spin as the ball changes direction.

Moving Up or Moving Back

If the bowler is coming up with a lot of splits and has attempted a change of line with no success, he may find that he has a timing error. This may be corrected by moving in to the pins if the ball is hitting too lightly on the headpin or by moving back if the ball is hitting too high (heavily).

Other Techniques

Another technique used by the skilled bowler is to change the speed of the ball he is delivering. Instead of changing the line of delivery, he simply slows up to increase the arc or throws harder to straighten the arc. This is a difficult technique to master, because in slowing down the ball you may lose some of the lift at release. In speeding up the delivery you may lose some degree of accuracy.

A few bowlers use two types of delivery — one to throw for the spare and another for the strike. Most often this happens in the case of the curve delivery on first ball and the change to a straight ball for the right side spares. Because the arc of the curve is so large, the ball breaks into the right-hand gutter. This big arc is ineffective on the right side approach spares.

Pin Bowling — Spot Bowling

There are two places on which the bowler may focus his attention. These two points of concentration are the spots marked on the lane and the pins. The hook bowler will find his spot at about the second arrow from the right, and the straight ball will be thrown at the same spot but on more of an angle. The curve bowler will adjust his spot to the size of the arc that he is throwing. The reverse hook bowler throws the ball out nearer to the third arrow so that it may cross and back into the 1-2 pocket. The advantage of throwing at a spot is that the range of vision is cut down to a smaller arc. With this smaller area come fewer distractive elements in the vision arc. Good peripheral vision increases the size of the vision arc, so a close target in this case is extremely important!

The pin bowling method amounts simply to looking all the way down the lanes to the pins. Advocates of this point of concentration say that looking further down the lane helps the bowler to throw out at the pins. This aids in getting good lift and action on the ball. In either technique the bowler should see the ball go over the spot or contact the pins. This is a part of the follow-through action of the bowler. The turn away from the pins occurs mentally four seconds before the turn; physically, it is initiated by small muscles two seconds before the turn, and then we witness the turn. It is important not to start this turn too early in the follow through.

When the bowler learns to study the lane, to find his place for rolling at strikes and spares, and to analyze his own delivery, he will become a skilled bowler. Long hours of practice are necessary for development of the skill and, thus, success.

TABLE 1. Mechanical Bowling Errors

PROBLEM	POSSIBLE CAUSE	CORRECTION
Dropping ball too soon	1. Weight on back foot at stance	1. Put the weight on forward foot; get arm motion started with step
	2. Ill-fitting ball	2. Purchase own ball
	3. Perspiration causes ball to slip	3. Do not put hands in ball too early
Arm doesn't have time for backswing	Pushaway is up and above head	Pushaway straight out or slightly down
Drifting (walking crooked)	1. Shoulders not square in stance; walk follows shoulder	1. Square up on the approach at stance
	2. Second step is away from midline of the body	2. Stride forward with second step
Running	1. First step too large	1. Shuffle on first step
	2. Incomplete arm swing; feet must catch up	2. Increase length of back-swing; add pushaway
	3. Off balance	3. Get feet apart on strides; do not lean too far forward at stance
Ball consistently to right gutter	1. Dropping ball too soon	1. Check ball fit
	2. Leaning back on release	2. Bend forward
	3. Timing off	3. Move up or back
	4. Dropping right shoulder	4. Square up shoulders parallel with foul line

TABLE 1. Mechanical Bowling Errors (*Continued*)

PROBLEM	POSSIBLE CAUSE	CORRECTION
Ball consistently to left gutter	1. Throwing cross body	1. Keep elbow close to body on backswing
	2. Turning thumb down and in on the release	2. Keep wrist firm
	3. Wrap around swing	3. Extend elbow on backswing
Throwing under the body and to left	1. Side of foot is parallel to foul line	1. Slide with toe pointing straight ahead
	2. Body twists to right	2. Keep shoulders square to pins
No power or roll	1. Lack of backward swing	1. Increase backswing
	2. No speed acceleration	2. Accelerate on second and third steps
Fouling	Approach too long	Shorten first step; start back farther
Lofting	1. Ball sticks to thumb	1. Check ball fit
	2. Knees not bent on slide	2. Bend to get nearer point of release
Skidding ball	Fingers and thumb releasing simultaneously	Thumb out of ball first
Ball breaking sharply left	Rotating wrist on release	Keep wrist firm and thumb in correct clock position
Pins fly straight back	1. Throwing too hard	1. Ease up
	2. Backswing too high	2. Cut down backswing
Pins fall lazily	1. Steering ball	1. Throw ball out farther over foul line
	2. No backswing	2. Push ball backward
	3. Dropped ball behind foul line	3. Get ball out; lift hand at release

4 □ Picking Up Spares

Naturally, the object of this game is to knock down all the pins with one ball, but for the beginning bowler this isn't always possible. Even the competitive bowler is excited about throwing five or six strikes a game. It is the rare bowler who throws 12 in a row. It is necessary in order to be a better bowler to learn to pick up the spares. Spare bowling is an art, and usually the technique is characteristic of the type of delivery the bowler rolls. There is one principle all bowlers might find easy to remember — **roll the best angle while using the most lane.** Below are the three angles from which almost all spares can be converted with just a slight body adjustment.

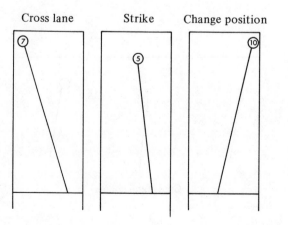

Cross lane   Strike   Change position

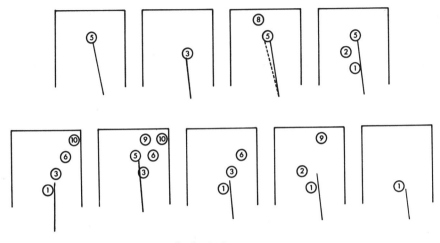

Strike ball spares

All these spares are rolled from the five pin angle shown in the foregoing figure. The delivery is that of rolling for the strike on the first ball. The feet do not
change position and the ball is rolled toward the center of the lane.

Cross lane spares are best accomplished by moving two or three boards to
the right with the left foot in the stance position. The bowler could also retain
his strike foot position but put the arm out at point of delivery to the right
slightly. Since the latter is difficult for the beginner, moving over slightly is
advised.

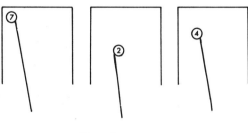

Cross lane spares

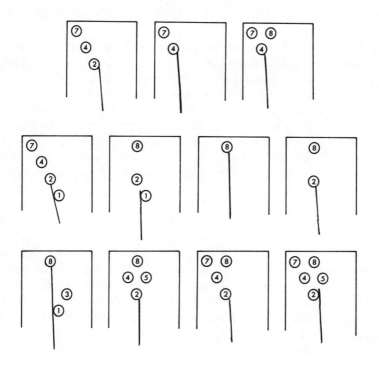

CHANGE POSITION SPARES

In converting these spares, the right-handed bowler moves to his left. The same delivery is used as was used for the strike spares and the cross lane spares. Sometimes bowlers attempt to roll one delivery for strikes and another for spares. To be consistent, use one delivery. On all the angles shown, the body should be facing the pins you are attempting to spare. Some skilled bowlers move the foot position on all the cross lane and change position for spares. They believe that it is better to move the foot position than to change the arm swing even a little. These bowlers roll more of a straight line delivery than an angle. Again, where you stand and how you throw depend greatly on your style of delivery. It is only through long hours of practice that you find your place and your spot. A bowler may bowl spares by looking at one of the spots on the lane or by looking directly at the pins. This technique must also be worked out by the bowler in a trial and error way until what is best for him is discovered. Eyesight, accuracy, and consistency play a large part in determining the point of aim.

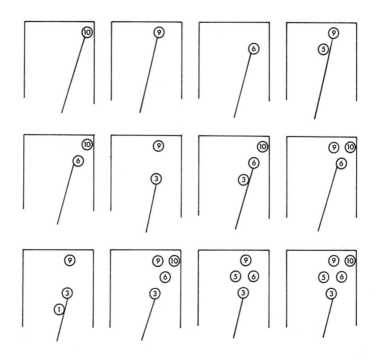

CONVERTING SPLITS

Splits are a result of hitting the headpin too high or too lightly. The lightly hit splits usually find the ball with little roll going into the headpin, hitting the pin, and backing off. The bowler who is consistently pulling high hits should increase the angle of his throw or check his delivery for faults in physical performance. There are some splits that are termed "impossible" splits. They really aren't impossible, but it is better for the beginner to aim for a sure pin or two. The following are difficult splits, and it is best for you to aim for the easy angle.

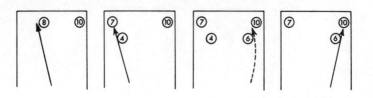

Baby splits

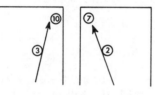

Exact splits

Example:

There are splits that are the exact split plus one pin. These must be made just as the exact splits are made, exact because the ball must fit perfectly between the two pins. If the ball rolls to the left or right a fraction of an inch, one pin will remain.

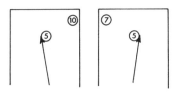

Woolworth splits

These are two common splits on a light hit. They probably come up in an evening's bowling as much as any other split combination.

3-6-9 METHOD

A scientific method for throwing the spare delivery is called the 3-6-9 method. The spot over which the ball must roll remains constant while the bowler's stance position changes. The bowler determines first his point of origination for the strike ball and from this point his stance position for converting spares. In this discussion we will consider the right-handed bowler with a hook delivery.

The most important part of the game of bowling is the ability to make strikes. To determine the spot on the approach from which the first roll will originate, the bowler goes to the twelve foot dots on the approach and lines the right shoulder up with the second range finder on the lane; this should put the feet close to the large dot on the center of the approach. This position will depend upon the size of the stride of the individual. The stance is taken each time from this point of origination, and the outside of the left foot is checked each time as the bowler takes his stance. The second range finder is on the tenth board from the right; the average-size person will find that if his right shoulder is lined up with the tenth board, then his left foot will be close to the eighteenth, nineteenth, or twentieth board.

The bowler should now walk straight toward his point of aim (the second range finder) and keep his swing, like that of a pendulum, close to the body. The approach should be smooth and the timing styled for the individual movement pattern. A bowler should change this point of origination only because of radically different lane conditions. The professional bowler works long hours to perfect his strike delivery and it is only this perfection of individual timing that can make anyone a champion.

When the individual does not get a strike, he must throw the second ball for the spare. The 3-6-9 method of moving to either the left or the right of normal strike position, depending on which pin is the key pin for making the spare, can help the bowler to choose the correct place to stand. The key pin is most often

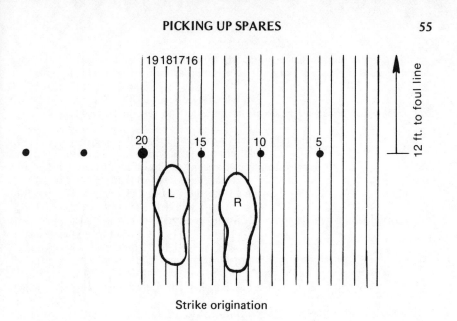

Strike origination

determined from its position on the lane. The closest pin to the bowler is generally the key pin, and after that determination, the bowler chooses one of the stances discussed below. However, splits sometimes make it impossible to follow the key pin rule and the bowler may want to check the charts on pages 52 and 53 concerning split conversion.

When the *two* pin is the *key* pin for making the spare, the bowler comes to the approach and lines the outside of his left foot three boards to the right of his strike stance position. Remember, the point of aim does not change but remains the second range finder.

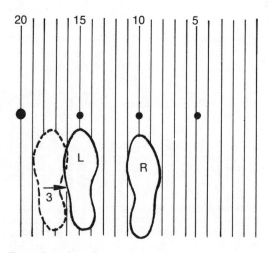

Two pin — key

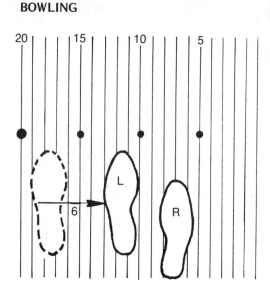

Four pin — key

When the *four* pin is the *key* pin for making a spare, the bowler comes to the approach and lines the outside of his left foot six boards to the right of his strike stance position. The point of aim remains the second arrow.

When the *seven* pin is the *key* pin for making a spare, the bowler places the outside of the left foot nine boards to the right of the strike stance position and throws at the second arrow.

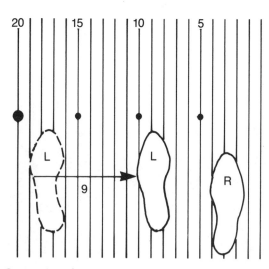

Seven pin — key

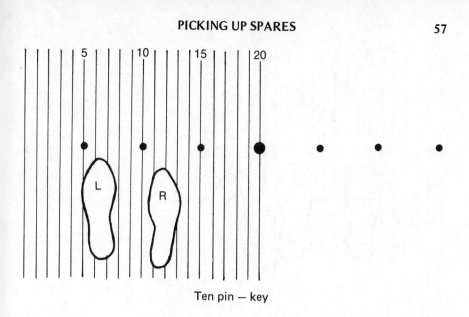

Ten pin — key

When the bowler wishes to convert spares on the *right* side of the lane, he begins with the *ten* pin as the *key* pin for the shot. The left foot is placed with the outside of the foot on the farthest dot to the left on the approach. The bowler selects the *third* range finder from the right as his point of aim and lines his body up with that point of aim and his target (the ten pin).

When the *six* pin is the *key* pin, the bowler moves the outside of the left foot three boards to the right of the ten pin stance discussed above. The third arrow is the point of aim.

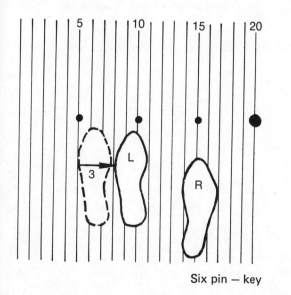

Six pin — key

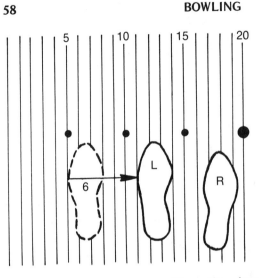

Three pin — key

When the *three* pin is the *key* pin, the bowler moves the outside of the left foot six boards to the right of the ten pin stance position and uses the third range finder again.

Earlier in this chapter, it was stated that the bowler, when attempting a spare, should "roll the best angle while using the most lane." This rule is the reason for using the third range finder as the point of aim for the right-side spares. The bowler gains the margin of error that allows him to make the spare on either side of the pin.

Some instructors think that the 3-6-9 method is difficult for the novice student to use, but in reality it gives the learner a more concrete idea of the point from which to originate each roll.

5 ☐ Scoring, Marking, and Handicapping

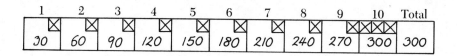

1	2	3	4	5	6	7	8	9	10	Total
☒	☒	☒	☒	☒	☒	☒	☒	☒☒☒☒		
30	60	90	120	150	180	210	240	270	300	300

SCORING

The game is divided into ten frames. A perfect game is a score of 300 – 12 strikes in a row. The highest number of pins scored in a frame is 30. There are three games to a match.

The *strike* is marked with a large X in the small box. Because all pins are cleared on one ball, the bowler is finished with this frame. The bowler in competition bowls this frame on one lane, the second frame on the second lane of the set, and so on, alternating lanes. The strike is scored as **10 + total of the next two balls.**

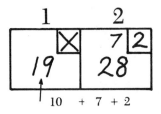

In the second frame the bowler hits seven pins on the first ball. On the second ball only two of the remaining pins are picked up, so the bowler has missed. The two balls should be marked as shown, because the scorer proves the number of pins the bowler has knocked down on both throws. The — (dash) is not used in the box of the second frame, although it is a miss or an open frame; the 2 is used to show two of three pins were converted.

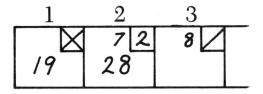

In the third frame the bowler hits eight pins on the first ball. He then picks up the remaining two pins for a *spare*. A spare is marked with a diagonal line. The spare is scored **10 + total of next ball.**

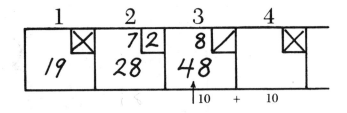

In the fourth frame the bowler scores a strike, so ten pins are added to the ten counted for the spare in the third frame. Again the score marker waits for two more balls before marking the score in the fourth frame.

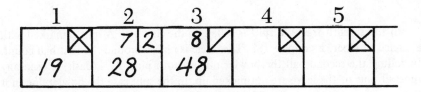

The bowler scores another strike in the fifth frame. Since two balls have not been rolled, the scorer still must wait to mark the fourth frame. Two strikes in a row are termed a double.

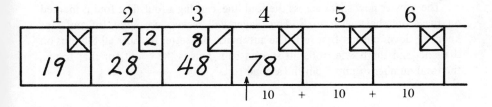

The bowler rolls a turkey — three strikes in a row. The scorer now adds for the fourth frame 10 + 10 + 10 (ten pins for strike in fifth and ten pins for strike in the sixth). A superstition in bowling would keep the scorer from marking anything until the bowler had finished striking. For the purposes of learning how to score we have marked the 78 scored in the fourth frame.

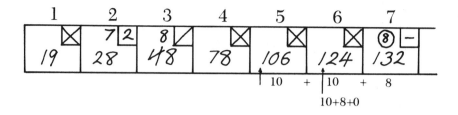

In the seventh frame, a split is rolled on the first ball. A split is marked with a circled number. Example: ⑧. The circle is placed around the first ball count. In rolling the second ball the bowler missed both pins. A — (dash) is used any time all pins of the leave are not picked up. In the split case the bowler does not have an error, blow, or miss. The bowler has only an open frame, one without a mark registered.

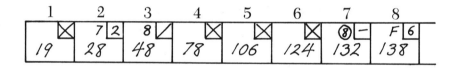

The bowler now slides across the foul line, causing a foul. The foul is marked on the score sheet with an F. The player will receive no credit for any pins knocked down on that first roll. The automatic pin setter replaces all ten pins on the lane, and the bowler rolls his second ball. This is the count for that frame, the total number of pins from the second roll.

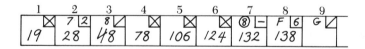

In the ninth frame a gutter ball is rolled and is marked with a G. Gutter balls are only marked G on the first ball. The bowler then knocks over all ten pins, but since it is the second ball, only a spare is gained. The scorer cannot mark the ninth frame until another ball is thrown.

The bowler "strikes out" in the tenth frame. In the ninth frame 10 is scored for the spare and 10 for the strike ball (first ball) rolled in the tenth frame. Remember, the scorer marks ten for a spare plus one more ball, not an entire frame.

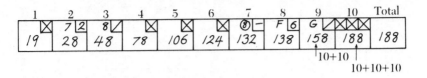

When a bowler makes a mark (spare or strike) in the tenth frame, he gains one bonus ball for the spare and two bonus balls for the strike. In every other frame two balls are the most rolled; in the tenth frame there is a possibility of three balls. If the first ball is a strike, two more balls would be due the player.

Review

Strike: all pins down one ball; 10 + two more balls

Spare: all pins down two balls; 10 + one more ball

Split: not a miss when not converted

Converted Split: split turned into a spare

Miss: no pins are picked up on second ball

Gutterball: on first roll, ball hits gutter before it gets to pins

Foul: no count for any pins down

Miss: two pins picked up of three remaining

Double: two strikes in a row

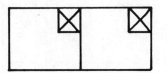

Turkey: three strikes in a row

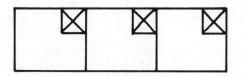

Strike Out: three strikes in tenth

A String:

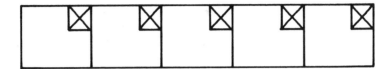

TEAM A

	1	2	3	4	5	6	7	8	9	10	
MARY (rolls)	8 /	X	9 /	X	X	7 | 1	9 | -	⑦ | 2	8 /	9 | -	
MARY (score)	20	40	60	87	105	113	122	131	150	159	159
BETTY (rolls)	7 | 2	8 | -	7 /	3 | 5	9 /	6 | 3	7 /	2 | 5	9 | -	8 / 6	
BETTY (score)	9	17	30	38	54	63	75	82	91	107	266
PAT (rolls)	⑧ | 1	9 | -	7 /	7 /	X	F | 3	9 /	8 /	4 /	6 | 3	
PAT (score)	9	18	35	55	68	71	89	103	119	128	394
CAROL (rolls)	5 /	⑦ | 2	X	6 | 3	7 | 1	8 /	X	X	7 | 2	9 | -	
CAROL (score)	17	26	45	54	62	82	109	128	137	146	540
TERRY (rolls)	6 | -	9 /	8 /	X	X	X	3 | -	9 /	6 /	8 / X	
TERRY (score)	6	24	44	74	97	110	113	129	147	167	707
Marks	2	4	9 ⁸	11	14 ¹⁶	19 ¹⁷	20 ²²	23	25		

TEAM B   + 39

	1	2	3	4	5	6	7	8	9	10	+ 39
JEAN (rolls)	8 | -	9 /	5 | 2	8 | 1	8 /	8 /	8 /	9 /	9 /	8 | -	
JEAN (score)	8	23	30	39	57	75	94	113	131	139	178
MARGE (rolls)	7 | 1	8 | -	8 /	4 | 5	X	6 | 4	9 /	⑦ | 2	7 /	8 / 5	
MARGE (score)	8	16	30	39	53	57	74	83	101	116	294
ELLIE (rolls)	6 | 3	5 | 4	7 /	8 /	7 | -	9 /	7 | 2	6 /	6 | -	- 6 -	
ELLIE (score)	9	18	36	53	60	77	86	102	108	114	408
SHERRY (rolls)	⑦ | 1	⑥ | 2	6 | 3	9 | -	5 | 4	8 | 1	6 | -	9 | -	5 | -	⑧ | 1	
SHERRY (score)	8	16	25	34	43	52	58	67	72	81	489
DOT (rolls)	X	X	X	X	X	⑦ | 2	8 | 1	9 /	7 | 2	8 / 7	
DOT (score)	30	60	90	117	136	145	154	171	180	197	686
Marks + 39 / 4	5	8	12 ¹¹	14	18 ¹⁷	19	21	24	26		

Sample scoring sheet

KEEPING MARKS

In competitive bowling the player likes to know how his team is doing as the game progresses as compared to his opponent. A person could total each frame and see, but a relatively easy system has been devised. The system is that of keeping marks. A mark is a spare or a strike; it is what we are counting in each frame and what we are comparing. The completed sample score sheet on page 66 will be used as our reference in the following explanation.

Rules of Marking

1. To *gain a mark*, it is necessary to make a strike or a spare.
Example: Mary has gained a mark for her team with a spare in the first frame. She gained another with a strike in the second frame.

2. To *gain two marks*, it is necessary to make two strikes in a row.
Example: Dot has gained two marks in the second frame with her double and two marks in both the third and fourth with her doubles.

3. To *lose a mark*, the bowler has rolled a *spare* followed by a count on the *next ball* of less than five.
Example: Betty has a spare in the third frame, but on her first ball in the fourth frame she knocks down only three pins. The bowler by this system loses credit for the mark gained in frame 3. Marge has done the same thing in the fourth frame.

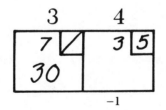

4. To *lose a mark*, the bowler has rolled a *strike* followed by a count on the *next two balls* of less than 5.
Example: Pat has a strike in the fifth frame followed by a foul and 3. The count for the foul is 0, and then Pat's second throw was for only three pins. A mark is lost to Team A in the fifth frame. Marge has done the same thing in frame 5 for Team B.

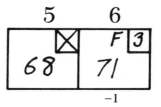

5. To *lose a mark,* a player has bowled two strikes and on the next ball has less than 5.

Example: Terry has a strike in the fifth and one in the sixth for a double. She rolls only three pins on her next ball, thus losing a mark for Team A.

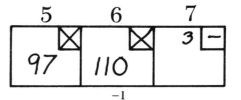

6. To *lose two marks,* a player with a double fails to throw more than five on the next two balls.

Example: Terry has actually lost two marks in the fifth because her total for the sixth frame was 3 on two rolls.

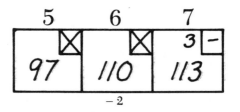

These rules have been established by a mathematician to allow the bowler to compare team scores. Each of them has a proof, which can be computed. These rules are used in competitive leagues to aid the bowler who is a keen competitor.

AVERAGES

A competitive bowler keeps an average of his weekly scores. Each week, when the bowler has completed three games, the league secretary adds these three games to all the other game scores already rolled. The total of these scores is divided by the number of games rolled for the bowler's current average.

Example: 118
            135
            172
            124
            140
            135
            165
            138
            140
            —————
            1267 ÷ 9 = 140.7

The bowler has an average of 140 with seven pins left over. The next time this player rolls in this league, he needs to roll only two pins per game over his present average to increase his average to 141.

Formula: Total of all games rolled divided by number of games rolled = current average.

The league secretary's record cards will look like this:

MARY BROWN				WIBC # 8807		
Date	Game 1	Game 2	Game 3	Total	Accum.	Aver.
2/14	118	135	172	425	425	141
2/21	124	140	135	399	824	137
2/28	165	138	140	443	1267	140

HANDICAPPING

In leagues in which the range of averages is wide, the league may adopt the handicap rule. The handicap is a method of "evening up" the chances for winning between opposing teams. There are three basic kinds of handicapping — the team base handicap, the individual base handicap, and the team total handicap. The league decides together at their organizational meeting which kind of handicap and which percentage of handicap they will use throughout the year. The Women's International Bowling Congress suggests percentages of 60, 70, 75, 80, or 90; the higher the percentage the more pins a team is given. The league must also decide upon a base score in cases in which the team base handicap system is used. The base score must be higher than what any bowler in league would have as an average. Since handicaps are not used in highly skilled leagues, it would be safe to adopt 200 per bowler as a base in any league. In some of the leagues with low averages, 150 or 180 might be selected as a base per bowler.

TABLE 2

TEAM A		TEAM B	
Name	Average	Name	Average
Mary	130	Jean	132
Betty	140	Marge	135
Pat	125	Ellie	110
Carol	135	Sherry	125
Terry	170	Dot	142
	700		644

Team Base Handicap (Using 70 Per Cent Handicap and 1000 Base for Five-Member Team)

Sometimes the base is referred to as scratch. Since there is another definition for scratch (score bowled without a handicap), we prefer in this book the term *team base*.

Example:

1000	base	1000	base
−700	Team A's average	−644	Team B's average
300		356	
× 70%		× 70%	
210	handicap each game	249	handicap each game

Team A will receive 210 pins each game they roll. Team B will receive 249 pins per game.

Individual Base Handicap (70 Per Cent Handicap and 200 Base Per Bowler)

In cases in which the bowler's participation may change from week to week, it is best to use the individual base handicap. This may occur in industrial leagues where men are working varied shifts or in leagues such as church leagues that are purely for social purposes. In figuring these handicaps, the secretary computes each week individual handicaps for all the bowlers on the team's roster. On the night they bowl, the five bowlers present add their handicap into their individual total per game.

Example:

Name	Average		
Mary	130	200	base
		−130	
		70	
		X 70%	handicap
		49.00	pins

For each game she bowls Mary adds 49 pins to her score. Each bowler on the team has a handicap computed that is added into her final score.

Team Total Handicap (70 Per Cent Handicap — No Base)

Example:

Team A Average   Team B Average
    700   644

$$700$$
$$-644$$
56 pins difference
X 70% handicap
39.2 pins per game added to all games
Team B bowls in match

The team total handicap is the simplest way for the league secretary to compute handicaps. In figuring the team base handicap, Team B was given 249 pins and Team A, 210. If you subtract the two, the difference is 39 pins in Team B's favor. There are also 39 pins given to Team B on the score sheet when the league uses a team total handicapping procedure. The mathematics is simpler, as you can easily see from the examples, when the secretary uses the team total. The other advantage is the cutting out of the base figure. The only advantage of the base method is that both teams get something. The handicap system is used in women's leagues mostly, but some men's social leagues also handicap.

Figuring Handicaps into Marks

To know where the team stands as they go along in the game, the handicap must be figured into the marks at the start of the game. Each mark is worth 10 pins minimum. In the team handicap the total number of pins given a team would be divided by 10. In our sample game, we used 39.

$$10)\overline{39.0} \atop 3.9$$

Team B would be given +4 marks* to start the game. This +4 is added to the marks in Team B's first frame. A total of 39 pins is added to the first girl's total as shown on the score sheet. In base handicapping, both first girls would have pins added to their scores and marks added to their team's first frame. Each score is added to the next for an accumulated total in the last box provided.

---

*If the number of marks had been 3.3, only 3 marks would be added. In figuring marks, 0.5 or greater is considered as the next whole number. This is the only time in scoring that the numbers are rounded off; all other times the less-than-whole number is dropped because it represents a part of a pin.

6 □ Rules and Etiquette

RULES*

Official Game

The bowling of ten complete frames on a pair of lanes on which the game was started shall constitute an official game, except that the league officers may authorize the completion of a game and series on another pair of certified lanes when equipment failure on the starting lanes would delay the normal progress of the series. An interrupted game and series shall be resumed from the point of interruption.

In league play, the first game of a series shall be started on the lane on which a team is scheduled. Succeeding games shall be started on the lane on which a team has finished the preceding game.

The members of the contesting teams shall successively, and in regular order, bowl one frame on one lane, and for the next frame alternate and use the other lane, so alternating each frame until the game is completed. Each player shall bowl two balls in every frame, except when he makes a strike.

When a player makes a strike in the tenth frame, he should be permitted to bowl two more balls on the same lane. When a player makes a spare in the tenth frame, he should be permitted to bowl one more ball on the same lane.

Score sheets shall not be mutilated or defaced in any way whatsoever. Scorekeepers should insert in small figures the number of pins secured on a strike and spare.

---

*These excerpts are taken from the WIBC Rule Book with the permission of the Women's International Bowling Congress. Most of the other rules in this publication pertain to league play. When a player joins a league, he receives a rule book upon payment of dues.

Legal Pinfall

Every ball delivered by the player shall count, unless declared a dead ball. Pins must then be respotted after the cause for declaring such dead ball has been removed.

1. Pins which are knocked down by another pin or pins rebounding in play from the side partition or rear cushion are counted as pins down.

2. If when rolling at a full setup or in order to make a spare, it is discovered immediately after the ball has been delivered that one or more pins are improperly set, although not missing, the ball and resulting pinfall shall be counted. It is each player's responsibility to determine if the setup is correct. He shall insist that any pins incorrectly set be respotted before delivering the ball; otherwise he implies that the setup is satisfactory. No change in the position of any pins which are left standing can be made after a previous delivery in order to make a spare, unless the pinsetter has moved or misplaced any pin after the previous delivery and prior to the bowling of the next ball.

3. Pins which are knocked down by a fair ball, and remain lying on the lane or in the gutters, or which lean so as to touch kickbacks or side partitions, are termed dead wood and counted as pins down, and must be removed before the next ball is bowled.

Illegal Pinfall

When any of the following incidents occur, the ball counts as a ball rolled, but pins knocked down shall not count.

1. When pins are knocked down or displaced by a ball which leaves the lane before reaching the pins.

2. When a ball rebounds from the rear cushion.

3. When pins come in contact with the body, arms or legs of a human pinsetter and rebound.

4. A standing pin which falls when it is touched by mechanical pinsetting equipment, or when dead wood is removed, or is knocked down by human pinsetters, shall not count and must be replaced on the pin spot inscribed on the pin deck where it originally stood before delivery of the ball.

5. Pins which are bowled off the lane, rebound and remain standing on the lane must be counted as pins standing.

6. If in delivering the ball a foul is committed any pins knocked down by such delivery shall not be counted.

Dead Ball

A ball shall be declared dead if any of the following occur, in which case such ball shall not count. The pins must be respotted after the cause for declaring such dead ball has been removed and player shall be required to rebowl.

1. If, after the player delivers his ball and attention is immediately called to the fact that one or more pins were missing from the setup.

2. When a human pinsetter removes or interferes with any pin or pins before they stop rolling or before the ball reaches the pins.

3. When a player bowls on the wrong lane or out of turn.

4. When a player is interfered with by a pinsetter, another bowler, spectator, or moving object as the ball is being delivered and before delivery is completed, the player must then and there accept the resulting pinfall or request that pins be respotted.

5. When any pins at which he is bowling are moved or knocked down in any manner, as the player is delivering the ball and before the ball reaches the pins.

6. When a player's ball comes in contact with any foreign obstacle.

Foul

A foul is committed, with no pinfall being credited to the player although the ball counts as a ball rolled, when a part of the bowler's person encroaches upon or goes beyond the foul line and touches any part of the lane, equipment or building during or after executing a legal delivery. A ball is in play and a foul may be called after legal delivery has been made and until the same or another player is on the approach in position to make a succeeding delivery.

If the player commits a foul which is apparent to both captains or one or more members of each of the opposing teams competing in a league or tournament on the same pair of lanes where the foul is committed, or to the official scorer or a tournament official, and should the foul judge or umpire through negligence fail to see it committed or an ABC approved automatic foul detecting device fail to record it, a foul shall nevertheless be declared and so recorded.

Foul counts as ball bowled

A foul ball shall be recorded as a ball bowled by the player, but any pins bowled down when a foul is committed shall not count. When the player fouls upon delivering the first ball of a frame, all pins knocked down must be respotted, and only those pins knocked down by the second ball may be counted. If he bowls down all the pins with his second ball after fouling with first, it shall be scored as a spare. When less than ten pins are bowled down on the second ball after fouling on the first, it shall be scored as an error. A player who fouls when delivering his second ball of a frame shall be credited with only those pins bowled down with his first ball, provided no foul was committed when the first ball was delivered. When a bowler fouls during the delivery of the first ball in the tenth frame and bowls down all ten pins with his second ball (making a spare), he bowls a third ball. When a player fouls while delivering his third ball in the tenth frame, only those pins bowled down in delivering his first two balls shall be counted.

ETIQUETTE

Almost all sports have a form of etiquette or good sportsmanship connected with them. Bowling is a sport in which courtesy and concern for the other player are reflected in the bowler's own success. Although the player may be competing against various teams, he is always competing against himself. Encouraging others on your team to roll well and praising good shots by all players show sportsmanship at its best.

Rules of Courtesy and Safety

1. Wear only regulation bowling shoes while bowling.

2. If you are using a house ball, be sure of the number of the ball and make sure you use the same number on all deliveries.

3. Do not ask to borrow another bowler's personal ball.

4. Do not bring food or drink into the scoring area or onto the approach.

5. When you are awaiting your turn, refrain from talking to the bowler on the approach. Loud noises may disturb the bowlers several lanes away.

6. Take turns keeping score.

7. Be sure if you are keeping score that you know what has happened to the bowler on his turn. Do not ask each time, "What did you do? Did you get that? How many pins did you get?"

8. Watch the bowlers on your own team roll, compliment them on a job well done, and give encouragement when it is needed.

9. Right of way
   a. Two bowlers approach at the same time; the player on the right goes first when they have the same set-up.
   b. The bowler with the spare goes first when the other bowler is on a strike throw.

    c. The split goes first in any case.

    d. Do not step onto the approach until the right of way is determined.

10. Be sure the rack has reset and the pins are up before rolling.

11. When you have finished rolling the ball, back off the lane. Be sure not to throw your arms, jump, or stamp on the approach. This is a distraction to the bowler many lanes away who has good peripheral vision.

12. Check to see, if you have a pinboy, that he has cleared the pit before rolling your second delivery.

13. Do not discuss lane conditions or personal mechanical difficulties. If you're having a bad night, work out your own problems. A "sour apple" can make the whole team fail.

14. Bad temper or tantrums have no place in this game.

15. It is always a tender situation when one bowler tries to tell another his error. Concentrate on your own game.

16. Relax and enjoy yourself; you will bowl better when you do!

7 □ Bowling Organizations

ABC

The American Bowling Congress was organized in New York State in 1895 after several unsuccessful attempts had been made to start a governing organization for bowling. The ABC set up rules and backed them with sanctioning and membership. The original group consisted of approximately 1000 members, mostly from the state of New York. At present there are about four million members from all over the country. The official organization has offices in Milwaukee, Wisconsin. The ABC is reported to be one of the most effective governing bodies in sports. The group has expanded to include the American junior bowler, the senior division for men over 55, and the collegiate division.

The ABC has a rule book, given to every member upon payment of annual dues, that covers everything from organizing and sanctioning of leagues to awards for high games and series that are rolled. The WIBC has adopted many of the rules that were written by the ABC Rules Committee.

Each year the standards for equipment are reviewed and new equipment is studied and tested. Constant inspection of lanes and enforcement of ABC regulations have insured that high standards are maintained.

The biggest event in bowling is the ABC tournament, which has run each spring since 1901. Teams come from all over the United States, Canada, and Mexico to compete in the events divided into three classes: the team event for teams with an average below 900, the team event for teams with over 900 average, and the masters' event for professionals. One of the outstanding events is the masters' in which spectators can see exciting players compete. The ABC has a Hall of Fame like many other professional sports, and new members are elected each year from the outstanding competitors. Each year the Bowling Writers' Association ballots to choose the "Bowler of the Year" award. Don Carter of St. Louis has won this award six times in the past 35 years. Other men who have won the honor more than once are Dick Weber of St. Louis (three times), Steve Nagy of Detroit (two times), Buddy Bomar of Chicago (two times), Ned Day of Milwaukee (two times), Earl Anthony of Dublin, Calif., and Nelson Burton of St. Louis.

WIBC

The Women's International Bowling Congress was organized in 1916 by 40 women. Today there are almost three million women members who bowl in WIBC-sanctioned leagues. Currently the WIBC, the ABC, the Brunswick Corporation, and the American Machine and Foundry Company are involved in a tremendous bowling promotion campaign.

The sister organization of the ABC also has a rule book, which is given to all members upon payment of dues. The national offices for the WIBC are in Greendale, Wisconsin. The WIBC tournament is held at almost the same time of the year as the ABC tournament but in a different large city in this country. This tournament, like that of the ABC, has produced many outstanding female participants. WIBC has a similar Hall of Fame, and the Bowling Writers select the outstanding woman competitor each year. In the past 30 years, Marion Ladewig, a grandmother from Grand Rapids, has won the award nine times and gained the title "Bowling's Most Outstanding Woman." Some of the women who have won the award more than once are Shirley Garms of Palatine, Illinois (two times), Sylvia Wene of Philadelphia (two times), and Val Mikiel of Detroit (two times). Over the past years, the five states that have consistently had the largest membership in the WIBC are New York, Ohio, California, Michigan, and Illinois.

ACU

The American College Unions usually sponsor the Collegiate Division for college bowling participants. The WIBC and the ABC provide Collegiate Division memberships to students enrolled in a college full time who wish to bowl competitively. The campus appoints a representative to the ABC and the WIBC, and this person then applies for league sanction. The campus representative must be a full-time administrative staff or faculty member.

The following are the rules of eligibility for collegiate bowlers who wish to participate in the ACU-I Tournament:

1. The bowler must be a Collegiate Division member of the ABC or the WIBC.

2. No college bowler can participate in a league in which money or merchandise prizes are given. This includes substitution or pacing.

3. No collegiate bowler can receive money for a commercial enterprise, such as endorsing products.

4. No collegiate bowler can accept a scholarship for bowling, such as those given for golf and tennis.

5. Each college may have a social or academic eligibility rule that must be adhered to.

6. The collegiate bowler cannot coach for money.

The WIBC and the ABC have established these rules to protect the amateur. The two organizations are looking forward to the day when bowling may be included in the Olympic Games. The WIBC and ABC offer awards of low monetary value to the college student.

The annual ACU-I tournaments are held in January and February in all the 15 regions of the country. The college man or woman who wins their regional all-events is then sent to the nationals held in conjunction with the ABC and WIBC Tournaments. During the regional tournament, each bowler must roll a team series, a double series, and a single series for a total of nine games. The total of these nine games represents the all-events score. One man and one woman from each region are eligible to compete in the national event. The winner from these 15 regional students then goes on to compete in the international tournament.

AJBC (YABA)

Many years ago the ABC promoted and organized the American Junior Bowling Congress for girls and boys interested in bowling. The age limit has no lower range (a bowler of five is registered), but the maximum age is 18. If the youngster elects to bowl in an adult league, he must give up his eligibility for the Junior Congress and must become a member of the adult group. The youngster may no longer enter any Junior League tournaments. Youths in these leagues are aided in competition by adult advisors. At present there are more than 800,000 AJBC members. We might compare these leagues to the Little League of baseball, except that these youngsters often score as well as their adult counterparts. The WIBC has added its support to the AJBC and helps organize tournaments and special events.

On August 1, 1982, the AJBC and YBA (the BPAA's Youth Bowling Association) merged to become the Young American Bowling Alliance (YABA).

BPAA

The Bowling Proprietors' Association of America consists of owners and operators of centers; most of them are also participants. Their annual meeting is usually held in conjunction with the ABC Tournament in the spring. At the meetings, lane specifications and conditioning are the main topics of discussion. New products are demonstrated and discussed. Selling the public on bowling is one of the most important aspects of the owner's job. Most BPAA-operated lanes sponsor special events throughout the year. They are also important in getting leagues organized and underway. Most centers run some kind of league participation all year round. The regular fall and winter leagues run from 30 to 35 weeks out of the year; there are also short-term spring and summer leagues.

PROFESSIONAL BOWLERS' ASSOCIATION

The Professional Bowlers' Association represents those persons who try to make their livelihood from the bowling game. The PBA promotes tournaments and special events and joins with other bowling enterprises to educate the public about bowling.

THE NATIONAL BOWLING COUNCIL

"The National Bowling Council is a non-profit service and educational organization formed in 1943 to consolidate and unite every phase of bowling. As national spokesman for the entire sport of bowling, the Council is dedicated to making bowling a truly lifetime family sport. During more than a quarter-century of activity, the Council has served bowling as publisher of manuals and kits, advertising coordinator, legislative liaison body, administrator of junior programs, film producer, public spokesman, and trustee for charitable groups in the game."[*]

THE LIFETIME SPORTS FOUNDATION

The Lifetime Sports Foundation was made up of a group supported by funds from contributions. Sports manufacturers, companies interested in sports, and organizations such as the ABC, WIBC, and BPAA gave this foundation large monetary gifts. Presidents John F. Kennedy and Lyndon B. Johnson gave strong support and added publicity to the program. The President's Council on Physical Fitness has also given its aid and promotion.

The main purpose of the organization was to promote individual sports that can be used as recreational outlets for a lifetime. One of the ways in which the foundation promoted was through its educational and instructional programs. The Lifetime Sports Foundation has produced for the American Association for Health, Physical Education, and Recreation a set of instructions for teaching bowling anywhere. Most of the states hold clinics for the junior high or high school teacher who needs help in working out an instructional program for the individual sports within his own teaching facility limitations. Promotion of this educational program by the foundation has done much to interest young people in lifetime sports as a means of developing and maintaining physical fitness.[†]

Although the thrust of this organization has diminished, it helped to train teachers at all school levels. These teachers have continued to apprise their students of sports which can be enjoyed after school and into adulthood.

---

[*]National Bowling Council, Washington, D.C., 20006. (The author worked for NBC from 1970 to 1975 as a consultant.)

[†]The author was a National consultant for Lifetime Sports.

8☐Tournaments and Games

TOURNAMENTS

Headpin Tournament

Once a year at the end of league play, a headpin tournament is held as a special event of a competitive league. The object of this event is to hit the head-pin with the very first ball thrown. The player is given 12 turns throughout the game; the highest possible score for a game is 120 and for the highest series, 360. In the series (three games) a perfect score is 360, but an excellent score is anything over 300.

The rules of bowling are observed except that there is only one ball per frame. The frames are not bowled on alternate lanes. The highest possible score in any given frame is 10; even doubles (two strikes in a row) or turkeys (three in a row) do not raise the 10 count. If the headpin is not hit with the ball, the score is 0 for that frame. The score is accumulated until 12 frames are bowled. If the headpin falls as a reaction from pin splash, the bowler is not given credit. The scorer must watch carefully to make that judgment.

Dutch Couples — Scotch Doubles Tournament

In couple leagues, a tournament called the Dutch Couples may be rolled. The man and the woman alternate balls and roll one game together. The frames are bowled on alternate lanes as in a regular game; a perfect game is 300. Again, all rules of the regular game are observed.

The woman usually throws the first ball and the man tries to spare her leave. If the woman throws a strike, her partner must wait until the next frame to roll. He rolls the first ball of the next frame and she must then convert the spare. The rule is to alternate people and alternate lanes. It is termed "Dutch" or "Scotch" because two are sharing one game. Three games are rolled in a series, and the high twosome wins the tournament. This event is usually the culminating event of the season.

House 200-250 Handicap Tournament

In some bowling centers, the management may sponsor a tournament at the end of the regular bowling season which is open to all women who have bowled a 200 game and to all men who have scored a 250 game during the regular league season. The bowler's final average is used, and the house sponsor sets a percentage handicap based upon the span of scores of people entering the tournament. The bowler rolls three games and adds in the computed handicap figure. The bowler with the highest three-game total plus handicap wins. Along the same line, a bowling proprietor may sponsor a scratch tournament for all women who have rolled 600 and for all men who have hit 650 in his center.

Team, Doubles, and Singles Tournaments

In a city, state, or national scratch tournament, the first event bowled is the team event. All bowling regulations are observed and all bowlers must belong to the ABC, WIBC, or AJBC. Some special rules for tournaments may be found in each of these organization's rule books. The second event is the doubles event in which two bowlers roll as a pair for a six game score. A team splits into two doubles pairs, and the fifth bowler is placed in a pool with all other fifth bowlers from participating teams. A pair drawing is held and these doubles teams are formed. The last event rolled is the singles event in which every man is for himself. There is a winning team, a winning doubles pair, a winning individual, and finally an all-events winner. The all-events winner is the person who scores high total for all nine games. This is the greatest of all honors because this individual has bowled consistently high in each of the events.

GAMES

Least Pins (Automatic Pinsetters)

This is a popular event on the first night of the ABC tournament. Two men roll for each team on opening night and attempt to knock down the smallest number of pins without throwing the ball into the gutter. The object is for the first man to knock down either the 7 or 10 pin and for the second man to put his ball in exactly the same place. The lowest possible score would be 1.

Thread the Needle (Pinboy)

Another first-nighter at the ABC is the Thread the Needle event. In this tournament, the entire team attempt to throw their strike ball between the Big Four split. The 4-7 and 6-10 pins are set, and all five bowlers try to throw a middle lane delivery that knocks down none of the four pins.

7 and 10 Shadow Game (Automatic or Pinboy)

This game can be played without pins, and in this case the scorer must judge whether the bowler has hit the pin. The bowler is given two balls each frame for ten frames, and 2 is scored as a perfect frame, 20 as a perfect game. The right-handed bowler attempts the 7 with the first ball and the 10 with the second. The game is made simpler with a pinboy who sets the two pins after each frame. The third way to accomplish the game is to have all the pins up and attempt to hit just the two with the two rolls. It is a little distracting to the beginner, but the skilled player should have enough concentration to play the game any of the three ways.

Blind Bowl (Automatic Pinsetters)

In Blind Bowl, a sheet is placed across the pins and the bowler looks only at the spots. The bowler on a spare relies upon the automatic pinsetter to light up standing pins so that he may know at which pins he is shooting. A regulation game is played and it is an excellent one for the practicing of spot bowling.

Progressive Splits (Pinboy)

This is a game for the skilled player who wishes to practice exacting deliveries. The bowler progresses through ten split setups in a game. Any split could be chosen, but below is a list of ten splits, progressing from the easiest to the hardest for a ten-frame score of 22. None of these is an impossible split.

1.	2-7	6.	5-7
2.	3-10	7.	6-7
3.	4-5	8.	4-10
4.	5-6	9.	6-10-7
5.	5-10	10.	4-7-10

Best Ball

This is a game similar to the one having the same name that is played by golfers. Usually two bowlers oppose two other bowlers in a single game. The game is bowled on a set of lanes and all rules are observed. The two bowlers of a team approach the lanes; first one bowls his first ball and then the other rolls. Whoever bowls the best ball and leaves the fewest pins will be scored. The two bowlers then decide who will attempt the spare. If a strike were rolled, no decision would be necessary; the strike would be scored. The second pair of contestants then go through the same process. Scores are usually very high in this game, and it is a favorite of television audiences who watch the pros attempt the game.

Gymnasium Games

Gym bowl

The Lifetime Sports Foundation sells a bowling kit for schools that is excellent for use indoors. All the games already mentioned can be played and practiced in a gymnasium before a youngster ever gets on the lane. The gym bowl kit contains ten regulation-size plastic pins and a light composition ball with regularly drilled holes.

Candlesticks

Candlesticks may be used very effectively in the gymnasium to practice the bowling skills. A light playground ball and the candlestick work very effectively in teaching rules and skills. The ball should be about the size of the indoor softball. Candlesticks can be ordered through local sporting goods stores.

* * * * * *

William Penn wrote the following to Hanna Callowhill in 1673.*

"We were at bowls yestereen, and though I got more pins at each first roll than my friend Anzi, yet so my score was less.

"They do reckon outrageously; for do I throw the nine pins with one bowl, and hit none at all with the remaining two, still do they account me the more skillful and do bestow a larger account than would fall to me did I strike them all with the three bowls.

"This wearies thee, but at my time the bowls themselves furnish a seemly and good diversion."

The many thousands who bowl for fun, for prizes, or to improve their health would agree with these statements. And so will you as you strive to master the many skills of this challenging sport called bowling!

---

*Courtesy of The American Bowling Congress, Public Relations Department, 1572 East Capitol Drive, Milwaukee, Wisconsin 53211.

Glossary

ABC — American Bowling Congress, the men's organization, which controls competitive play and promotes tourneys.

Alley — Term for the bowling house or for just the lane.

Anchor — Last and best-under-stress bowler on the team.

Approach — The area in front of the foul line on which the bowler stands to make delivery.

AJBC — American Junior Bowling Congress, the sibling organization for young people. Replaced in 1982 by the YABA (Young American Bowling Alliance).

Baby split — A 3-10 or 2-7 leave after first ball of frame.

Big four — The 4-7-6-10 split.

Blind — A score given a team for an absent bowler.

Blow, error, miss, open — Failure to pick up a possible spare.

Bocce — Italian game similar to bowling.

Bridge — The distance between the two finger holes on the ball.

Brooklyn — Ball hitting to the left of a headpin for right-hander.

BPAA — Bowling Proprietors' Association of America, center owners.

Bucket — The 2-4-5-8 or 3-5-6-9 leaves.

Build a foundation — A ninth frame strike.

Candlesticks — A bowling-like game played on the East Coast.

Center — Current term for a bowling establishment.

Cherry — To pick off one pin on a two pin spare.

Chop — To pick off one pin on a three or four pin stand; also may be used to mean cherry.

Count — The number of pins knocked down with first ball.

Cross lane — Bowling from the corner and crossing the center of the lane.

Curve — A ball that begins to make a large arc to the left the moment it is thrown.

Dead ball — A ball that results in little pin action.

Dead wood — Pins that have fallen on the first ball thrown.

Double — Two strikes in a row.

Duck pins — A miniature bowling game, ball held in hands.

Dutch 200 — Alternate strikes and spares through a game.

Explosion point — Point at which the ball leaves the hand with an upward lift.

Fast lane — A highly polished lane; straightens out the arc on a curve or hook delivery.

Foul — Physically crossing the line dividing the lane bed and the approach.

Frame — A division of the game; each game has ten such scoring divisions.

Full hit, high hit — Hitting the headpin squarely on the nose on first throw. Also called on the button.

Gateposts, goalposts — The 7-10 split.

Graveyard — A set of lanes with which a bowler has difficulty.

Gutterball — A ball that goes into the gutter before it hits the pins.

Handicap — A score adjustment used in competition to equalize the opportunity for opposing teams to win.

Headpin — The pin numbered 1.

Hook — The ball that veers sharply to the left just before reaching the pins for the right-hander.

House — The bowling establishment or center.

Kegler — A German term for bowler, still in use.

Kick — A pin that rebounds off the sides of the end of the lane.

King pin — Began as 5 pin because of its center location and stirring ability. Some people refer to the headpin also as the king, because it is desirable to hit this pin for a strike.

Lane bed — Area from foul line down to the pit.

Lead off — The first bowler on the team; most often the second high scorer on the team.

League — An organized group bowling on a regular schedule.

Leave — The pins still standing after the first ball.

Lift — The upward motion of the fingers at point of release.

Line — To bowl a line is to bowl ten frames.

Lofting — Throwing a ball too far out on the alley.

Mark — To mark is to get a strike or a spare.

Open — A frame in which there is no mark. It is not always a miss because the leave may be a split.

Picket fence — The 1-3-6-10 or 1-2-4-7 leave.

Pin action — The reaction of one pin against another; the splash.

Pit — Place at the end of the lane bed in which pins fall and are reset.

Pocket — The space between the 1-3 pins for right-hander; 1-2 is the pocket for left-hander.

Pushaway — The forward motion of the arms coordinated with the first step.

Railroad — A split.

Reverse hook — Sometimes referred to as a backup because of the backspin placed on the ball at release.

Rolling english — A ball that has a lot of spin imparted, a mixer.

Roundhouse — A curve with an extremely large arc.

Scratch — Bowling without benefit of a handicap.

Sleeper — A pin standing directly behind another pin. Example: 2-8, 3-9.

Slow lane — One that allows the hook or curve ball to bend easily.

Spare — Getting the remaining pins with the second ball.

Split — Headpin is down with at least two pins standing and pins are missing from between those pins. Headpin is down and there are just two adjacent pins standing.

Spot — The mark on the lane at which the bowler aims.

Strike — Knocking down all the pins with one ball.

Striking out, going all the way — Three strikes in the tenth frame.

Sweeper — A first throw that literally sweeps the pins away.

Tap — A perfectly thrown strike hit that leaves a pin.

Thin hit, light hit — A ball that barely knocks over the headpin on the first roll; sometimes even results in strike.

Timber — The pins.

Turkey — Three straight strikes.

Washout — The 1-2-4-10 or 1-3-6-7 spare.

WIBC — Women's International Bowling Congress, sister organization of the ABC.

Woolworth, five and dime — The 5 and 10 split.

YABA — Young American Bowling Alliance, the youth divisions of the ABC, WIBC, and BPAA. Started in August 1982, incorporates the junior organizations of the ABC and WIBC (AJBC) with the similar group run by the BPAA proprietors (YBA).

In no other sport, except possibly football, are there so many terms connected with the activity. To feel at home in this sport it is necessary to recognize and use the language. Because this was the sport of the average man, the terms connected were mostly slang phrases concocted to suit the situation. It is another part of bowling that gives it "color" and makes it a popular pastime.

Selected References

BOOKS

Barnes, Mildred, Fox, Margaret, Loeffler, Pauline, and Scott, M. Gladys: *Sports Activities for Girls and Women.* New York, Appleton-Century-Crofts, 1966, Chapter 6. (This text provides a brief discussion of bowling practices.)

Bellisimo, Lou: *The Bowler's Manual,* 3rd Edition. Englewood Cliffs, New Jersey, Prentice-Hall, Inc., 1975. (A thorough discussion of technique by a master bowler.)

Gym Bowl – Instructional Manual. AAHPER, 1967. (A teacher's manual for planning lessons.)

Kalman, Victor: *Natural Bowling.* New York, Permabooks, 1961. (A paperback with good description of technique and added comic relief.)

Mackey, Richard T.: *Bowling,* 2nd Edition. Palo Alto, California, Mayfield Publishing Co., 1974. (An excellent text for the beginner.)

Martin, Joan, and Tandy, Ruth: *Bowling.* Dubuque, Iowa, Wm. C. Brown Co., 1980.

National Bowling Council: *The Bowling Instructor's Handbook.* Washington, D.C., 1974.

Pin Pointers. Milwaukee, Wisconsin, ABC, 1968. (A manual written by professionals for American Bowling Congress.)

Stanley, D. K., et al.: *Physical Education Activities Handbook for Men and Women,* 3rd Edition. Boston, Allyn & Bacon, Inc., 1973. (Brief bowling discussion.)

Vannier, Maryhelen, and Poindexter, Hally Beth: *Physical Activities for College Women,* 2nd Edition. Philadelphia, W. B. Saunders Co., 1969, Chapter 6. (A book for students in required college classes, with discussions of many sports.)

MAGAZINES

Bowling (American Bowling Congress). Greendale, Wisconsin, American Bowling Congress. (An excellent monthly magazine for keeping up with current happenings.)

Woman Bowler. Greendale, Wisconsin, Women's International Bowling Congress. (The magazine for current happenings with women bowlers.)

RULE BOOKS

American Bowling Congress Rule Book, published annually.
Women's International Bowling Congress Rule Book, published annually.

FILMS

American Bowling Congress, 1572 E. Capital Drive, Milwaukee, Wisconsin. Fifteen films available.

American Machine and Foundry Company – Bowling Division, Jericho Turnpike, Westbury, New York. School Instruction Bowling Course Kit (slide film included).

Brunswick Corporation, 623 Wabash Avenue, Chicago, Illinois. Bowling Instruction Course Kit, five color slide films.

SLIDES

Learn to Bowl, Gilbert Altshul Productions, Chicago, Illinois, 1971.

TRANSPARENCIES

Bowler Development Program, Prentice-Hall and Robert J. Brady Co., 1969.